Do you need relief from your hassles?

At times, all teens think their problems are more than they can handle. Your family...your friends ...even your own feelings can get you down. This book addresses the struggles that all young people face. Dr. Collins knows your problems are real and understands that you can't wait forever to find solutions. Whatever pressures you face, here is your opportunity to handle any situation by using a direct, scriptural approach.

GARY R. COLLINS

GIVE ME a BREAK!

Power Books

FLEMING H. REVELL COMPANY
OLD TAPPAN, NEW JERSEY

I am grateful to Steve Snyder of Taylor
University for his suggestions and help in the
preparation of the study guide.

Scripture quotations not otherwise identified are from The Living Bible,
copyright © 1971 by Tyndale House Publishers, Wheaton, Illinois. Used by
permission.

Scripture quotations identified NIV are from HOLY BIBLE New International Version, copyright © New York International Bible Society, 1978.
Used by permission.

Excerpts from UNHAPPY SECRETS OF THE CHRISTIAN LIFE by
Philip Yancey and Tim Stafford. Copyright © 1979 by Youth for Christ International. Used by permission of the Zondervan Corporation.

Excerpts from THE TROUBLE WITH PARENTS by Tim Stafford.
Copyright © 1978 by Youth for Christ International. Used by permission of
the Zondervan Corporation.

Material by Ann Landers is used by permission of Ann Landers and the
Field Newspaper Syndicate.

Excerpt from Dawson McAllister's "America's Teenagers: Misery in the
'Me' Generation," *Worldwide Challenge,* February 1980, is used by permission of Dawson McAllister.

Library of Congress Cataloging in Publication Data

Collins, Gary R.
    Give me a break!

    "Power books."
    Study guide: p.
    Bibliography: p.
    Includes index.
    Summary: A guide for teenagers on how to handle stress
caused by such things as peer pressure, parents, school, family
problems, emotions, sex, and religion. Each problem is
examined and discussed from a Christian viewpoint.
    1. Youth—Conduct of life. 2. Youth—Religious life.
[1. Conduct of life. 2. Christian Life. 3. Youth—
Religious life] I. Title.
BJ 1661. C628 1983   248.8'32   83-21289
ISBN 0-8007-5153-1

To
my favorite teens
Marilynn
Jan
Dwane
Chris
Rochelle

Contents

1

Making the Best of Stress

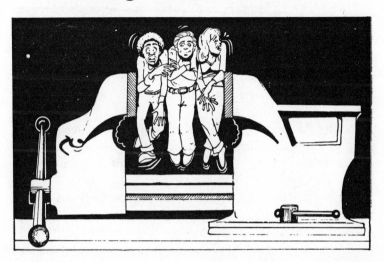

They call it the "suicide belt"—ten wealthy towns strung together along the shore of Lake Michigan, north of Chicago.

The teens who live there aren't poor. Many of them go on family vacations to Europe or the Caribbean, live in huge houses with swimming pools, and sometimes even drive the family Mercedes to school.

But a lot of these kids are miserable! Suicide attempts are common, and once or twice a month somebody succeeds.

Maybe it isn't surprising that the filmmakers of Hollywood chose the suicide belt as the setting for the powerful movie *Ordinary People*. It told the story of Conrad Jarrett, a frustrated teenager who lived in a home where the parents were insensitive and too busy. His father was caught up in business and probably uncertain about how to handle a teenage son. His mother was selfish and more concerned about status than about other people.

The kids at school were unsympathetic, and Conrad was struggling with guilt over his brother's death and hurting so much inside that he reacted the only way he knew how.

He slashed his wrists!

Things are worse in the ghettos, of course, but that's where so
many people are poor, sick, mistreated, and without much hope.
In the suburbs of places like Chicago, New York, Atlanta, or San
Francisco and in the little communities further away from big
city centers, things are supposed to be better. The air is clean.
The neighborhoods are neat and quiet. The people are more
friendly.

So why do so many teens feel unhappy—some even to the
point of attempting suicide?

One answer is *stress*—that constant tension of living in a world
that puts everyone under pressure.

Almost all of us feel it—teachers, parents, businessmen, and a
host of others—but in some ways teens have it worse. Moving
into adulthood has never been easy. You're still trying to find
yourself and you don't have the money, power, experience, or
know-how to cut through the tension and get what you want.
Peer pressure can be very powerful, forcing you to make really
difficult decisions about drugs, sex, cheating, alcohol, jobs, and
even religion. With so many parents having problems themselves
or filing for divorce (and sometimes even turning to their children for advice and comfort) it is common for teens to feel left
out, pushed aside, hurt, neglected, angry, guilty, and confused
about both marriage and adulthood. Then some teacher tells you
to study harder or presses you for a decision NOW about next
semester's courses—courses which might decide whether you'll
get into college and which could even influence your eventual
choice of a vocation. Added together, stresses like these can be
almost overwhelming.

Not everybody responds like Conrad Jarrett, of course, but
you probably know at least one person who has almost buckled
under building pressures. I have a friend, for example, who

barreled into high school, bursting with excitement and enthusiasm. Almost immediately she was ridiculed by upperclassmen, put down by teachers, and overwhelmed by the demands of assignments that were hard and had to be done on time. She felt trapped and helpless, and tensions at home added to her frustration. Before long she was depressed and disillusioned. It wasn't easy for her to change, and it took a long time before she recovered her old sparkle.

When tensions build up like that, it doesn't help much to know that teen stress has been around for centuries. You're living *now!*

It isn't very comforting to realize that the pressures may be greater in other countries. You live *here!*

It probably doesn't mean much if you are warned that alcohol and drugs only dull the stresses for a while but can have devastating consequences later. You've got to do something to ease the tension *now!*

So maybe it *is* encouraging to know that stress can be handled.

You can understand it.

You can reduce it.

You can control it.

Stress doesn't have to overwhelm you or lead to the desperate solutions tried by those kids in the suicide belt. You can learn from stress and live a better life in the future because of what you learn.

If you feel overwhelmed at times, join the crowd! This book has been written to help people like you handle stress. It is meant to be interesting. Most of all, it is intended to be helpful.

What Causes Stress?

Several years ago some teenagers at a midwestern high school got on the phone and reported a fire. When the police and firemen arrived in great haste, the kids took advantage of the confusion by jumping into a squad car and driving away. They had a wonderful time cruising around the streets with the siren going until they ran out of gas. Then they ditched the car, hopped on a bus, and went back to school.

As you might guess, the school officials weren't amused by this stunt, and the police at that time were too embarrassed to press charges. (All of this was later reported widely in newspapers, so the police in your area probably are aware of this incident and would likely get tough with anyone who tried it again!) The squad car joyride came to the attention of some psychiatrists, however, and the good doctors decided to do a big study to find out what teenagers are really like.

Armed with questionnaires and psychological tests, these researchers began the long process of talking to 20,000 American teenagers—in ninety different high schools—and they added another 2,500 interviews in Israel, Australia, and Ireland. As you would expect, some of these students were rebellious and delinquent. Some were emotionally disturbed, and others were physically ill. But the overwhelming majority were very normal. Most of them were coping pretty well with the stresses of life.

It was also found that these teenagers had a great interest in trying to understand themselves, their friends, and their parents. Maybe you too have wondered why people feel and act the way they do. Have you ever considered how we can get along better with others? What makes some people religious? How do we reach conclusions about right and wrong? What are the best ways of coping with pressure?

Before we can answer questions like these, we first must understand what causes stress. Most of it comes from three sources: other people, frustrating circumstances, and inner turmoil—the things that make you feel uptight.

Let's consider *people* first.

If you were to stop reading for a minute and list the five most common stresses in your life, what would they be?

Not long ago I asked a group of teens to make such a list, and their answers were interesting. Most of the pressures came from parents, brothers and sisters (especially younger brothers and sisters), other teens, teachers, and people at work.

It probably would be worse if we were completely alone on some deserted island. Having people around at least keeps us from getting lonely. But people can also cause problems and create tension. Each of us is unique. We have such different interests, experiences, tastes, beliefs, and viewpoints that it is almost impossible, at times, to avoid clashes and disagreements with others. Sometimes people bother us, ignore us, criticize us, or push us to do things that we might prefer to avoid. All of this creates pressure. If we want to reduce stress, therefore, it is clear that we will have to learn how to get along with others.

A second cause of stress is what we might label *events*—the things that happen to us. Think how frustrated and pressured you feel when you study all night but then get a D on the test in the morning. You join the football team, work hard at all the practices, and then spend a whole season sitting on the bench. You try out for cheerleading and don't get chosen. You can't find a job—or you get fired from the one you've had. You take driver's education, pass your test, and then have almost no opportunity to drive the family car. You wait all year for a big school party and then sit home because you don't have a date. All of these are frustrations caused by disappointing events in our lives.

Frustrations arise whenever we fail to get something that we really want. You don't need a book to tell you that this happens often, and it doesn't help much to realize that most of life is filled with frustration. Sometimes we respond by getting mad, discouraged, or "down" on ourselves; but the frustrating events are still there, and they continue to create a lot of pressure.

Another cause of stress is the problem of inner turmoil—the *uptightness inside* that is so hard to handle. Have you ever known someone who was friendly, popular, and seemingly had it all together, but who then surprised everyone by attempting suicide late one night? Such people usually struggle with conflict inside themselves, but they manage to keep everything hidden from others.

If we are honest, most of us would admit that we have inner battles—even though we may never even think about suicide. Consider, for example, the inner fears most people feel at some time: fears of failing, of being rejected or disliked, of not being able to please our parents, of being turned down for a date, or of not getting into college.

If you are like most people, you have inner concerns about yourself—the worry that you may be too ugly, too stupid, too poor, or too unpopular to succeed. You know the inner discouragement which comes when you can't get along with your parents, fail in school or athletics, can't understand algebra, don't get a date, or are unable to find a summer job. Consider, then, the inner battles you may have over sexual thoughts and struggles. Think of the times when you felt an inner guilt over something you had done—or not done when you should have. Then give some thought to the inner confusion many people have about religion or about what our standards of right and wrong should be.

Add to these the inner struggles about where to go to college, how to choose a career, or what to do about peer pressures, and we have a list which could really get you down.

Recently I saw a book on a newsstand that surely expresses the feelings of many people. The title was *How to Survive Being Alive.* I've never read the book, but I know we survive by recognizing that stress comes from three sources: other people, frustrating events, and uptightness inside. In every stage of life we can learn how to live in the midst of pressure. Once we know this, we have taken a big step forward in learning to handle our problems.

How Do We Handle Stress?

You probably are reading this book because you want to find some better ways of handling your stresses, but you already know some things about reducing tension. Depending to some extent on your past experiences and personality, you have learned that sometimes it is helpful to cry, to look for something to laugh at in the midst of your problems, to talk them over with a friend, or to pray. Perhaps you've also tried less successful things, such as getting mad and lashing out at people, running away, pretending the problems don't exist, or trying to escape from them with drugs or alcohol.

There are some other approaches, however; things which may be common in you or your friends. We don't always see these in ourselves, but at one time or another most of us use the following ways of handling stress.

The dreamer reaction to life's problems is to escape into our own little world of fantasy. For some people this most often happens when they are bored—in school, in church, at work, or even on vacation. At such times we dream about how life could be better or we imagine that we are rich, famous, successful, attractive, out from under the influence of parents, able to get even with some-body we don't like, or married to a famous person. This kind of daydreaming can be an interesting diversion, of course, but it can be overdone, especially when people spend so much time dreaming that they don't honestly and realistically face the challenges and problems of life.

The complainer reaction is seen in people who are always griping. Somebody has called these people "grievance collectors." They constantly find fault with parents, teachers, work, kids at school, and anything or anybody that gets in the way. Sometimes in their minds, complainers pile up lists of annoying things and then use this stockpile of gripes as ammunition for the next argument. By criticizing everyone else, the complainer feels better and thinks he or she comes out looking like the only person who is "number one" and without faults. Regretfully nobody else shares this opinion: Complainers are not very well liked, and the person who always gripes as a teenager often turns into a bitter, sour adult. Most teens have heard this dozens of times, but there is an old saying that really makes sense: If you can't say anything nice, don't say anything at all.

This can also apply to your thinking. If you think complaining thoughts all the time, your attitude can become sour. On the other hand, life is a lot less stressful if you think about things that are true or beautiful and let your mind dwell on what is good and admirable in others.

At times we all complain—it's probably a built-in part of our human nature. But life is a lot more pleasant if we can resist the tendency to criticize. When we don't resist, the problems expand in our minds and the stresses often seem a lot worse than they really are.

The brooder reaction to stress is seen in people who say little but mull problems over in their minds. These people aren't necessarily complainers, but they spend hours thinking how unfair things are and how terrible life can be. Sometimes the brooding pulls them down so much they become depressed and even suicidal. *Then there is the joker reaction to stress.* We all know people (perhaps you are one of them) who laugh at everything, joke a lot, and don't seem to take life very seriously. Such people are often very popular "party types" who attract a lot of attention and may be well liked.

But the mask of humor frequently hides people who are unsure of themselves, who may be afraid of closeness, and who use humor to avoid the painful task of honestly facing life's problems.

I know something about these people because that's how *I* tried to act as a teenager. I was really struggling with a lot of inner fears, but nobody knew this. It was so easy to laugh off any serious discussion and to hide behind a big phony front that said, "Isn't life fun—isn't it great to be so happy and well adjusted!"

Please don't jump to the conclusion that there is an aching heart behind every smiling face. That isn't always true, but excessive joking can sometimes be a way of avoiding stress.

Another way of handling stress is the charmer reaction. This was described beautifully in a Christmas card we once received. A mother wrote that her six-year-old daughter was seeing a child psychologist who said that the little girl had a "case of the cutesies."

I know some teens—and even a few middle-aged adults—like that. They are oozing with charm and somewhat babyish in their mannerisms (especially when they feel uncomfortable or are under stress). Although they may be very capable people, they give the impression of being empty-headed and uncertain about how to act their age, so they respond like little kids.

Lori (that's not her real name—I don't want to embarrass anyone in this book) was a teenager when I first met her. She was good-looking, a stylish dresser, not a bad student, and she had a good part-time job. People liked her because she was so charming and friendly, but she got silly whenever stress built up. She rarely could get close to people because they thought she was immature and sometimes suspected that she was using her syrupy charm to manipulate others. Being cute had helped Lori in the past whenever things got tense. When she grew up she forgot to leave her childish ways behind. Probably she didn't know any better way to act. I wonder if Lori had met people who use the next reaction?

The explainer reaction to stress involves having an answer (excuse might be a better word) for everything. When these people are late it's someone else's fault. When they fail a test it's because of the teacher, because there was no time to study, or because of a noisy younger brother who made it impossible to concentrate. When they are arrested on a drug charge they blame the problem on their upbringing and find some logical reason to explain why drugs are in the car.

Probably everybody gives excuses at least sometimes, and usually these reasons are at least a little true. By giving a good explanation for our actions we win the approval of others and avoid the stress which comes from being criticized. Regrettably, we sometimes stretch the truth in order to provide a better explanation. That's a subtle form of lying. Sooner or later that gets us into trouble.

The avoider reaction is an ostrichlike way of handling problems. Instead of burying our heads in the sand, we escape into a world of television, novels, sports, hobbies, or even religion. This lets us forget our problems and pretend that they don't exist. But they do exist and they continue, even though we may try to forget them.

Hardly anyone would say that television, sports, or the other diversions are all bad. They can provide relaxation and be a good diversion for a while, but they also can take all of our time or energy so that we fail to face our problems "head-on."

The actor reaction is a way of avoiding stress by putting up a front or pretending to be something that we aren't. When his dad was killed in a car accident two years ago, Rob pretended (perhaps even to himself) that the loss didn't mean much. Working on the assumption that "eighteen-year-olds don't cry," Rob showed no emotion at the funeral and tried to carry on as if nothing had happened. Months passed before he faced his grief honestly and freely admitted that he was lonely, angry, and very sad.

Perhaps Rob learned something that many teenagers suspect—the world is filled with actors. These may be very sincere people, but their money, success, family ties, and calm, well-adjusted exteriors hide the fact (sometimes even from themselves) that inwardly they are hurting and weighed down by stress.

A very different approach is the tackler reaction. Like football players who hit the opposition with force and determination, some people face their stresses honestly and try to do something about them.

Sometimes, however, we don't know what to do. Nobody has told us how to handle doubts, peer pressure, career decisions, troublesome emotions, or problems with parents. That is why the following chapters have been written—to help you be a better stress-tackler.

As you read, I hope you also will discover the benefits that come from the believer reaction.   When they reach their teenage years, many people begin to question their religious beliefs and those of their parents. In the midst of this struggle, however, a new awareness of God often emerges. There is a recognition that the God who created us also understands, protects, cares for, and helps us with our stresses, even though we might not think very often about His influence.

Which Way Is the Best Way?

When I first presented this list of reactions to a group of teen-agers, somebody asked a good question: "Which is the best way to react to stress?"

The answer is that no one of these reactions is best or worst. Most people use all of the reactions at one time or another, although we tend to have favorite ways of responding. We soon learn that all these reactions to stress do help, but they can also create more problems than they solve. When we rely completely on these ways of handling problems (except for the tackler and believer reactions), we use a lot of energy avoiding our problems instead of facing them honestly and trying to solve them.

There also can be danger in using these tactics too much. They are ways of denying the reality of stress, and when the denial continues, the stresses can build in you, as they build in the kids on the suicide belt.

It makes sense to admit that you have stresses like everybody else. Be honest enough to realize that we all tend to avoid unpleasant situations for a while, but real solutions only come when we *do* something about our specific stresses.

The next ten chapters deal with some of these specific stresses. We'll begin by considering how we can meet the stress that comes from trying to get along with other people.

2

People Stress: Getting Along With Others

I'm not sure how Mike ever found his way into church. His family certainly wasn't interested in religion, and Mike didn't seem interested either.

Nevertheless, we met on the church steps. He was standing next to the pastor, who had asked whether I could counsel with Mike about his problems in getting along with people.

In his fifteen years of life this young man had managed to get into trouble with just about everyone. He didn't get along with his parents, had no friends at school, and hated his teachers. When I met him, he was in trouble with the law because he had hit a policeman who was trying to break up a fight.

Not many of us have this much trouble getting along with others, but it is rare to find a person who relates well to everyone.

What psychologists call "problems in interpersonal relations" bring about labor-management disputes, squabbles among politicians, many crimes, and even wars. Because they are unable to get along, parents argue and sometimes separate, students have disputes with teachers and with each other, brothers fight with their sisters, and parents are often in conflict with their children. To live with such strife is painful; to resolve the tensions and get along smoothly is not easy—and sometimes impossible.

Getting along with another person requires effort, especially when you don't like that other person or when he or she doesn't seem to be interested in getting along. Have you ever had a teacher or employer who delights in being nasty and apparently is disinterested in you—even though you are trying hard to please?

All is not hopeless, however, because getting along with others is a skill that can be learned. As with bicycle riding or ice skating, some will learn faster than others and some will be more skilled. By remembering a few basic rules all of us can reduce a lot of the stress that comes from our contacts and conflicts with other people.

Rule No. 1: Ask yourself, How am I a part of the problem?   You don't need a college degree to know that it takes at least two people to fight or have a disagreement. When you don't get along with someone else it is easy to be a blamer who tries to shift all responsibility onto others.

Jesus once talked to a man who was like that. His father had died and he and his brother were arguing over the money that was left. "The problem is my brother," the man told Jesus. "Please tell him to divide everything fairly." Instead of getting into the family fight, however, Jesus told the man to stop being greedy. Apparently the chief complainer was also the chief problem.

That might not be true with you. Sometimes other people really *are* the biggest cause of your problems, but it is always helpful to ask what *you* might be doing or thinking that makes matters worse and keeps the conflict alive.

Do you criticize others, for example, especially when they aren't present? Sooner or later they are likely to hear about your criticisms, and that hardly builds "warm-fuzzy" relationships.

Do you yell, make sarcastic comments, use belittling gestures, or make facial expressions that are sure to irritate?

Do you refuse to cooperate, to listen, to talk, or to forgive?

Do you stubbornly demand your own way and refuse to compromise?

Have you failed to realize that every person is unique and that some people have personalities which differ from yours? We get into trouble when we expect other people to be just like us.

I hope this doesn't sound like a lecture. That's the last thing that any of us needs. We don't get along better with others just because somebody tells us to shape up, and none of us likes to be told that our attitudes or actions could be part of the problem.

We have been raised in a self-centered society, however. We have all learned to be concerned about ourselves so it is easy to be selfish, greedy, and unforgiving. At times we demand our own way, hold grudges, and (for reasons which sometimes may be very good) refuse to trust some people. All of this can prevent us from getting along with others.

In His famous Sermon on the Mount, Jesus warned:

> "Others will treat you as you treat them. And why worry about a speck in the eye of a brother when you have a board in your own? Should you say, 'Friend, let me help you get that speck out of your eye,' when you can't even see because of the board in your own? Hypocrite! First get rid of the board. Then you can see to help your brother."
> Matthew 7:2–5

To get along with brothers and other people, the first step is to ask ourselves, *What might I be doing to make the problem worse?*

If you're like me, you can't always answer that question. Sometimes I snap at my kids and don't even realize it until my wife tells me. Often it helps to have an understanding friend who can point out what we are doing that might be keeping tensions alive—even if the conflict has been started by someone else.

What are the people-problems in your life right now?

Are you doing anything to make matters worse?

What could you do to change?

Do you have a friend or counselor who could help you see the problem more clearly?

Honest answers to these questions can help you deal better with people stress.

Rule No. 2: Try to see the other person's point of view. Someone has said that rock music must have been created to divide teens and their parents.

Such a statement shouldn't be taken too seriously, I suppose, but most teenagers' homes have had at least some discussion—perhaps heated discussion—about the quality and loudness of the music preferred by each generation.

When our kids were born, I decided that if they heard only classical music like that of Beethoven, Bach, and Brahms they could never stray into a preference for anything else. When they were babies, our children heard a few classics like "Baa, Baa, Blacksheep" and "The Farmer in the Dell," but most of the time they heard symphonies. In church they learned "Jesus Loves Me," but at home we played Bach chorales and Handel oratorios. Finally they reached the teenage years, got their own radios, and *guess* what they listened to—rock music played at full volume! So I threw out my stupid theory about how people learn a preference for music.

It wasn't long before problems arose when we would ride together in the family car. Only one radio could be played at a time (at least before the kids discovered earphones). Our teenagers didn't share my taste in music, and their mother and I weren't enthusiastic about theirs. I announced that we would make a democratic decision with five votes for me (since I'm the father), two votes for their mother, and one for each of the two kids. Clearly that didn't go over too well, so we began some long family discussions about lyrics, sound levels, rhythms, and the lifestyles of performers.

I still don't like most rock music, but some of it isn't too bad, and I'm learning to look at it from the teenager's point of view. My teens, in turn, have tried to understand my middle-aged way of seeing things, and all of this has made life much more pleasant. In the car we take turns now—sometimes rock, sometimes Bach—and at times we turn the radio off altogether.

Whenever conflicts come along it is easy to jump to conclusions about the other person's point of view without listening or trying to understand. Teenagers have opinions about such things as dating, hair length, entertainment, school, and movie stars. Parents sometimes have different opinions, and so may teachers or friends at school. It may not be possible or even desirable for you to accept another person's point of view (or for someone else to accept yours), but you can try to understand how others think. When you do this, there is a basis for respect, working out compromises, and reducing the stresses that arise as a result of your disagreements with people.

Rule No. 3: Work on communicating.   It should be easy for one person to give a clear message to someone else, but such communication is one of the hardest things in the world to accomplish. Every year advertisers spend millions of dollars trying to communicate with people, including teenagers, about products that are for sale. Politicians spend hundreds of hours trying to communicate. Teachers and (dare I say it?) writers work hard to communicate with students—and often fail. Married couples sometimes find communication so difficult that they give up. And everyone knows that some parents can't seem to give clear, unemotional messages to their children. Is it surprising, therefore, that you have some communication problems?

If you want to communicate well, start by listening carefully.

That is the first lesson new counselors learn and it is something that could help us all: Keep your big mouth shut—and learn as much as you can by listening to the other person. This means, of course, that you hear and try to understand the words that are being said, but it can also help to watch gestures or facial expressions and listen to the speaker's tone of voice.

In your house, how many times has there been a disagreement, perhaps even an argument, because one member of the family responded to what he or she *thought* somebody else said? When we don't listen we often find ourselves getting mad when there is no reason to do so. When we listen carefully we are less likely to jump to the conclusions that start little wars.

But good communication also means that you state your own views clearly and honestly. That is not easy, either!

Have you ever had a teacher who was brilliant, but whose speaking was clear as mud? No matter how hard you listen, such people can't be understood because they don't know how to speak good, clear English.

It's unlikely that you can change people like that, but at least you can try not to be like them. If necessary, speak slowly (especially when you have something important to say) and choose your words carefully.

Also, try to keep emotions under control. You are more likely to have an explosion if you shout, nag, call people names, criticize without clear facts to back you up, or use loaded words like *you always* or *you never*. When we get mad, we often say things we don't mean, and that just adds to the fight. King Solomon once wrote: "A soft answer turns away wrath, but harsh words cause quarrels" (Proverbs 15:1). The old king must have known what he was talking about. According to the Bible, he had 700 wives so he must have had a lot of practice in learning to communicate. A soft, gentle answer might have been his proven approach.

There is one more comment that should be made about communication: Don't send double messages.

A double message comes when you say one thing but give another message by your actions. My teenagers might be confused, for example, if my words say, "I love you and like spending time with you" but then I am always too busy to be with them (that's the message that could come from my actions). Actions speak louder than words, but it is best if actions and words are giving the same message.

If you know someone who says one thing but does something else, gently point out this difference. Then be sure that you don't do the same thing. Telling your parents, boyfriend, or girl friend one thing and then doing something different is a form of lying. That certainly doesn't improve communication.

Rule No. 4: Try to reduce other pressures and distracting influences. Have you ever tried to have a serious talk with someone in a restaurant where there is loud music, a waitress who keeps interrupting, the clatter of dishes, and a hundred people all talking at once?

I have been to Hong Kong on several occasions. I love the place, but that city contains some of the loudest restaurants in the world. Imagine yourself sitting at a big, round table talking to your friends, while apron-clad Chinese ladies walk by pushing carts of food and shouting above the noise so everyone will know what delicacies are for sale. The food can be delicious and the atmosphere is fun, but that is no place for a quiet conversation. McDonald's, Denny's, or Burger King may be a little quieter, but wherever there is noise and confusion, it is hard to give your full attention to the important task of getting along with someone else.

Noisy restaurants are not the only distractions, however. When you are worried about an exam, concerned about a dating relationship, afraid that you might get dropped from some team, or preoccupied with any other problem, it is difficult to keep your attention on getting along with people.

Around our kitchen table we recently had a discussion about a girl whom I'll call Sue. She had been a good friend of both my daughters, but suddenly Sue had become demanding, critical, hard to get along with, and impatient. It didn't take long for us to discover the reason for this personality change: Sue's parents were getting a divorce, and she was caught in the middle. All of her energy was used in coping with the stress at home. She had trouble studying, and it certainly was difficult for her to work at getting along with people. More than anything else Sue needed understanding and acceptance. When she found it in her friends she was able to cope better.

Sometimes you will be the one who needs to be patient with other people when they can't do much about the pressures of life. Try to be understanding and not demanding, at least while the pressure is on. Such an attitude can do a lot to reduce stress.

Remember, too, that some distractions and pressures *can* be removed. You can talk in a quiet place, for example, or wait until after a big exam if you want to communicate in a meaningful way.

Rule No. 5: Recognize God's power to help. The Bible talks a lot about peace, and it is clear that God wants us to get along with each other. Surely He wouldn't encourage this if getting along were impossible.

Saint Paul, who wrote much of the New Testament, was aware of many squabbles in the early Church. He urged the Christians to "be at peace" with each other, but then he did something more. He prayed.

We can follow Paul's example, and, like him, we can expect that God will hear our prayers and guide us. Do you ever ask God to help you get along better with your parents, employer, teachers, friends, or even people whom you dislike? Prayer, accompanied by some of the rules listed in this chapter, can be a powerful force in overcoming people stress.

Rule No. 6: Recognize that some conflict will not disappear. Most of us know at least some people with whom we may never get along well.

Let me mention Saint Paul one more time. He once wrote: "If it is possible, as far as it depends on you, live at peace with everyone" (Romans 12:18 NIV). Does this mean that sometimes it isn't possible to get along with others?

Some people use various tactics to keep arguments alive. They may, for example, call you names, refuse to discuss a problem, talk behind your back, or look for people who will side with them against you. You may try to defend yourself, to be nice, and to do whatever else you can to get along. Just as it takes two people to disagree, however, it takes two to solve a problem. If you try to smooth things over and the other person does not cooperate, you may have to accept the fact that, at least for now, the tension will last.

So what do you do then? Do you "grin and bear it," pretending not to care while someone else criticizes you and spreads rumors about you?

The answer is no!

Keep trying to get along with your critic.

Never stop treating the other person kindly.

Don't let him or her entangle you in an argument. Don't criticize the person in front of others but, at the same time, don't be afraid to give your side of the picture to people who might be influenced by your critic's viewpoint.

Remember, too, that God can intervene and bring peace later, even though that seems unlikely now.

Not long ago I wrote a college textbook on the subject of counseling. Just a few weeks after the book was published, it was criticized severely in a magazine article written by a man who doesn't seem to like anything I write. I suppose I could have fought back, but it seemed better to let the criticism pass. Before long other people came to my defense, and the views of that critic soon were forgotten. Do you remember King Solomon's advice? Sometimes a gentle answer, or even no answer, is the best way to deal with people who seem unwilling to change.

This brings me back to my friend Mike, whom I met in church.

I wish I could tell you that Mike learned to get along with every-one and never had any more conflicts with people.

That didn't happen! Mike decided that he didn't want to hear the suggestions given in this chapter, even though other people have found that they really work. Instead Mike was more con-cerned about getting even with the people who had wronged him. One day he didn't show for our counseling meeting, and I never saw him again.

I hope Mike eventually learned how to get along with people. Others have learned this important lesson, and I know you can too.

3

Peer Stress:
Handling Pressure From Others

Have you ever taken one of those psychological tests that asks you to complete a sentence? Usually they want you to fill in the blanks after words like these:

- What bothers me most is _____
- I like _____
- Women _____
- When I feel pressured _____
- The kids at school _____

Not long ago, I took one of these tests. When I saw the words *The unhappiest time_____*, I wrote the following sentence: *The unhappiest time in my life was when I was a teenager.*

There were a lot of reasons for my unhappiness. I wasn't a very good student (B at the best). I wanted to date but was too scared to ask and didn't have a car. Since I didn't drink or tell dirty jokes it was hard to be a member of the "in group" at school. I liked watching sports events but was so uncoordinated that when they picked teams in gym class I always was chosen last. I had few friends at school and faced a lot of tension at home.

The only bright spot in my teenage years was our church youth group. There I had friends and felt somewhat accepted, but I was younger than most of the other kids and it was embarrassing to be a little overweight. The fact that I was clumsy too sure didn't help to reduce my feeling of being left out whenever there was a softball game.

As we get older, it doesn't seem as bad to be a misfit, but when you are a teenager and unsure of yourself, it is very important to be accepted. When we aren't sure that we fit, when we are pressured to do things that we know are wrong, when we feel there are no other kids who understand us, and when friendships become a problem, then we are faced with peer stress. At such times there are several things we can do.

We Can Cop Out

Often there is value in withdrawing and getting away by yourself at least for a while. Some of the most creative, capable people in the world have been loners who pulled away from others during the teenage years and learned to become better athletes, musicians, or students. As a teenager, I buried myself in photography, developed a lifelong interest in reading, and succeeded so well in some part-time jobs that at times I still think about going to work in a department store like the one where I worked as a shoe salesman.

If we withdraw for a long time, however, we often feel lonely and sometimes begin to wonder if we are misfits. These feelings remind us that having friends is very important, so we start spending more time with others and return to the task of trying to get along better with our friends.

I once saw this in a teenager named Mitzi, a gymnast who wants to be in the Olympics. I know she'd like to spend more time with her friends at school, but most of her spare time is spent in practice. Everybody realizes that she's good. She's won a number of trophies and someday she might even win a gold medal. But it's lonely practicing by herself, and Mitzi has been missing out on a lot of the good experiences that can come to teenagers. She's beginning to wonder if the acclaim which might come as a gymnast in the future is worth withdrawing from people now.

Pulling away from others can be overdone. Like Mitzi, we each can withdraw into our own little world, dreaming about the future, and even working to succeed, but missing much of the present. Like some adults I know, we can also make the mistake of living in the past, thinking about the good old days and ignoring the stresses and responsibilities that come now. It certainly is fine to plan for the future and to have good memories of the past, but to get along in this world we must learn to fit into the here and now. We must learn how to deal with peer pressures, feelings of rejection, ridicule, and the many stresses that come from other teens. Copping out can be refreshing for a while, but it can lead to an extreme withdrawal from others. This just avoids the problem of peer stress. Nothing is solved.

We Can Compete

Instead of withdrawing from peer stress, many people have decided to compete.

This is common in well-developed countries and, certainly, it has been built into Americans and Canadians. Our parents and teachers have encouraged us to compete for awards, trophies, athletic victories, and attention from others. In school we learned to compete for grades and for places on the cheerleading or football squads. We compete in intramural sports and in band, choir, and athletic competitions between schools. Competition even gets into the church, and it dominates many homes when family members compete with one another and sometimes with other families.

As a male, I still am surprised whenever someone asks me to write an article for a woman's magazine. Not long ago it happened again. I was asked to write about competition. "Women run into a lot of competition," the magazine editor said. They see their husbands competing at work, their kids competing in sports, and their neighbors competing with each other. Women who work encounter competition on the job, and sometimes they compete silently with other women by trying to be superior homemakers, by pushing the kids to excel, or by working for a place of importance in the church or neighborhood.

But what about you? Are you caught up in the competition that someone has called "the killer instinct"? At times competing can be fun, exhilarating, and ego-boosting—especially if you win. But that is the problem with competition—there are both winners and losers. When you lose a race, a game, a contest, or a girl (or guy) you can feel deeply discouraged, very unhappy, even devastated. Most of us can understand why big, burly football players sometimes cry like babies in front of a whole crowd of spectators when their team loses an important game. Losing can hurt.

Bob Cousy was a professional basketball player—an all-time great whose skill and coordination amazed everybody who watched him play. But in a book about his career Bob Cousy admitted that the competition created indescribable tension. Competition is "both curious and frightening," he wrote. "The more you win, the more you need to win." The drive is never satisfied. In their push to succeed, many athletes become wound up, unable to relax or study, impatient, unfriendly, and sometimes snobbish.

This tension isn't limited to athletes. Competition in any area can be challenging and exciting, but it can lead to pride and a lack of concern for other people. Even when we win, the happiness can fade quickly, leaving us with feelings of emptiness and the same old problem of trying to handle peer stress on a day-to-day basis.

I know some adults who are always competing—most often with other adults, but sometimes even with their own children. These competitive people have never learned an obvious lesson that could make their lives a lot less miserable: Nobody can do well in everything. Some are good athletes, others are not. (How I wished my gym teachers could have understood that.) Some can swim well; others are nervous about even trying to stay afloat in a boat! Some are brilliant students; most of us are not. Some excel in music, mathematics, art, or writing, but many more people do not. While we all have some abilities and should concentrate on doing the best we can, we will all lose in some areas of life—and that needs to be accepted.

Philip Yancey, who formerly edited *Campus Life* magazine and who understands teens as well as anybody, wrote about his own struggles with winning and losing in *Unhappy Secrets of the Christian Life*. It might help if you read his words carefully.

Competition grabs us and squeezes until all we can think about is winning.... As I thought about it, a haunting question arose inside me.... What if all my schemes to compete, such as walking over Hal (a pudgy, sloppy, bookworm who was running for student body president), thinking myself superior to poor people on the bus, driving for success, really were futile? Many of the most successful people were not happy, that was certain....

Jesus was the opposite. His values were not based on school offices or wealth or status or being cool. After all, he had no home, no money. He was deserted by his friends and executed by his countrymen. Yet he won somehow. He fulfilled his mission on earth. His life turned the world upside down, even though he never walked over someone to do it. . . .

None of the things my friends and I worried about mattered to God. Looks, intellect, strength, status, ability—they made no difference at all. How could we impress the Creator of the Universe? Only one thing mattered: whether I gave myself to him and obeyed him. His way is hard, yet it is strangely fair: no one is excluded on the basis of talent or competition. We merely exclude ourselves by choosing against God. . . .

I still get depressed after a poorly played tennis match, and I know I will strive to do my best at my job. The difference is that earlier I was living for myself and I competed by beating out other people. I looked good in contrast to them.

Now, however, the only audience that counts is God.

God does not see us as misfits and neither does He accept us only if we win. God loves each of us, with no strings attached. I don't think He is opposed to our competing in sports or school, but when we hurt others in order to win, gloat in pride, look down on losers, or spend our whole lives wrapped up in competition, God is not pleased because He knows that this hurts everyone, especially ourselves. He makes each of us unique with our own gifts and abilities. He wants us to do the best we can in our various life activities. But Philip Yancey is right: The only audience that really counts is God.

Maybe you're like me. A lot of the competition in my life is really in my own mind. I start comparing myself with other people, wanting very much to be as competent, successful, good-looking, or capable as they are. I don't know this for certain, of course, but probably many of these people whom I so admire are really unsure of themselves, and they might even be competing with me.

Wouldn't it be less stressful to thank God for what I've got and then spend my energy trying to do better, *without* "putting down" someone else? I've even learned that such an attitude lets me sincerely be glad when someone else wins. That removes a lot of people stress.

We Can Conform and Compromise

Perhaps nothing puts teens under as much stress as peer pressure. Everybody knows that teens like to dress the same (that's being stylish), to do the same things (that's being "with it"), to talk the same jargon, to listen to the same kinds of music—preferably loud enough to drive parents crazy. Sometimes we form little groups (*cliques* is probably the more accurate word) and if you're "in" you can feel really secure with your friends. If you're "out" it can hurt, especially if you are handicapped, criticized, ignored, not invited to parties, or made to feel rejected.

Only once in my life did I agree to go on a blind date. We were going out with another couple, and when they revealed the identity of my date I almost had a heart attack. Shirley was in my class at school. She had buck teeth and no chin. I knew she was a nice person with a pleasant personality—but she was ugly. I shuddered to think how people would react if they saw me with her. When there were so many good-looking girls around would people think that Shirley was the best I could find or persuade to date me? Since I couldn't think of any way to retreat, we went out together, but I spent the whole evening trying to make it look as if Shirley and I really were *not* together.

I cringe now when I think of how that girl must have felt. She wasn't pretty (that's the understatement of this book), but she was intelligent and certainly must have known that she was a misfit in terms of her looks. Maybe she was lonely, rejected, and struggling with low self-esteem. That often happens when we feel left out.

Since it hurts so much to be left out or laughed at, a lot of us will do almost anything to be accepted. Think of what happens, for example, when you hear a joke that you don't understand but which leaves everyone else laughing. If you're like most people, you laugh too, because you don't want to be different or to admit that you don't "get it."

Several years ago some psychologists designed an interesting experiment to study peer pressure. Seven teenagers sat in a room and were shown cards that looked like this:

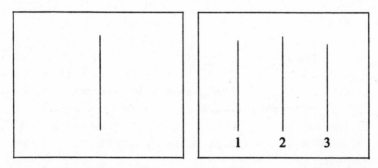

The teenagers were asked, "Which line in the box on the right is the same length as the line in the box on the left?" The answer of course is number 2, but before the experiment began, six of the teenagers were told to answer "number 1." How would you feel if you had been the one person in the room who didn't know the secret? Number 2 is clearly the right answer, but if everyone else said "number 1" would you go along with the crowd?

Almost 75 percent of the people tested did just that. When asked about it later, most admitted that they had used excuses to talk themselves into going along with the group. *Maybe I don't understand the instructions,* some thought. Others decided that something must be wrong with their eyesight. Those who resisted the peer pressure and said what they thought had a lot of discomfort and didn't like being different.

I should tell you one other thing about this experiment. If one other person in the room went against the group opinion, it was a lot easier for the teens to say what they really thought. Having a friend who agrees with you can really help you resist peer pressure.

How does all of this apply to us? Perhaps we can agree on three conclusions:

First, peer pressure is tremendously powerful and very hard to resist. It is easy to give in and join the crowd when everyone else is swearing, taking little pills, drinking beer, or smoking marijuana. It isn't easy to stay out of bed and to keep your virginity when everyone else says they are "doing it," and when they make you feel like a misfit who is odd, stupid, or "chicken."

Those people who can't resist peer pressure have trouble accepting those who *are* able to say no. When they go along with the crowd they lose their uniqueness, and it is uncomfortable for them to see that some people don't always buckle under pressure. If they don't ignore or reject you, they turn up the pressure with the same old argument that the devil used with Eve: "Try it— you'll like it!"

This brings us to our second conclusion: When the pressures build, we often find excuses that let us give in. We tell ourselves, for example, *Since everybody is doing it, it probably is okay; Nobody would know if I gave in; It wouldn't be so bad if I only did it once;* or *To give in would be a good way for me to understand how people in this world really feel and act.* Somebody has defined temptation as "a voice in your head that tells you reasons why you should go ahead." When we have a friend or two who can help us, it is easier to fight the excuses and resist the temptation. When we are alone or are being urged by others to give in, it is harder to resist.

When we do give in, we lose. That is the third conclusion. We may lose our virginity or our uniqueness, but we also lose our self-respect. Often we are plunged into guilt, afraid that we might be discovered and forced to lie about our actions. Every time we give in it becomes harder to resist when temptation comes again, and before long we start to look like chameleons.

A chameleon is a lizard that can change its color to match the surroundings. I know people like that and you probably do too. They fit into church meetings, sex parties, family picnics, Bible studies, pot parties, X-rated theaters, and evangelistic rallies. Jesus didn't call such people chameleons. He called them hypocrites. No teenager likes a hypocritical adult. Is a teenage hypocrite any better?

What do we do, then, about peer pressure? How can we handle the desire to be accepted without giving in and doing what is wrong? It isn't always wrong to cop out, compete, and conform, but sometimes these can lead to hypocrisy, pride, immature self-centeredness, and unkindness to others. Is there a better solution to peer pressure? The answer is clearly yes.

We Can Build Christian Maturity

The Bible has some interesting words about peer pressure: "Don't copy the behavior and customs of this world, but be a new and different person with a fresh newness in all you do and think . . ." (Romans 12:2).

To resist pressure and to keep from copying the standards of this world we can take five approaches to peer stress.

Expect it.   To live in this world is to expect pressure. Even hermits have pressures because they have to live with their own inner conflicts and loneliness. If you realize this, you are not so surprised and overwhelmed when the pressures build.

I know some preachers and youth speakers who seem to think that Christians somehow can escape problems. Teenage audiences are told that with Christ, life will be problem-free. Such an idea certainly doesn't come from the Bible. ". . . Here on earth you will have many trials and sorrows," Jesus told his followers, "but cheer up, for I have overcome the world" (John 16:33). To be warned like this should help you resist. That gets us to a second approach to peer stress.

Resist it.   How do we do this? Would it surprise you if I suggested that resistance begins with your mind? When we are

tempted, when we are afraid of being laughed at, when we hear
or start thinking about the reasons for giving in, when we get
concerned about being misfits—all of this starts in our minds. So
shouldn't we use our minds to resist?

Several years ago my wife and I invited a teenage relative to
come into our home and live with us for a while. Often when we
got into discussions about drugs, my young friend talked with
sadness about his friends who were "hooked." He gave some
very convincing arguments against drug use, but several months
later he had become a drug user himself.

What happened? He knew all the facts and dangers, but apparently he forgot all of this under the influence of peer pressure.
If we are going to resist, we need to constantly be asking ourselves, *Is this what I really want?*

Resistance, as we have seen, is easier when there are friends to
help. Remember that experiment with the teenagers looking at
lines? Although peers can be a bad influence, often they can be a
good influence—helping each other to resist pressure. Think of
this if you ever decide to go on a diet. It's easier when there is
someone else who cares enough to check up on you and to help
you avoid cheating. Friends can help in other areas too.

To be honest, we must recognize that most of us aren't strong
enough to resist on our own. That's where God comes in. If
you're like most people, these words from the Bible will seem
very realistic:

> Be careful. If you are thinking, "Oh, I would never be-
> have like that"—let this be a warning to you. For you too
> may fall into sin. But remember this—the wrong desires
> that come into your life aren't anything new and differ-
> ent. Many others have faced exactly the same problems
> before you. And no temptation is irresistible. You can
> trust God to keep the temptation from becoming so strong
> that you can't stand up against it, for he has promised this
> and will do what he says. He will show you how to escape

temptation's power so that you can bear up patiently against it.

1 Corinthians 10:12, 13

When temptation builds up, including pressure from others, we can ask God to help us resist and expect that He will do what He has promised.

Counteract it. Sometimes the best way to resist temptation is to replace it with something better.

Do you ever find yourself getting critical and bitter—perhaps angry at other people who are making your life so miserable? Instead of mulling over the faults of others and moaning about our own weaknesses, it can be helpful to ". . . Fix your thoughts on what is true and good and right. Think about things that are pure and lovely, and dwell on the fine, good things in others. Think about all you can praise God for and be glad about" (Philippians 4:8). The Apostle Paul wrote these words while he was in jail, with every reason to think angry, bitter, nasty thoughts. Instead he saw the value of thinking in ways that are positive.

It also helps if we can act in ways that are kind and which build people up. In the long run they respect us for this and appreciate our encouragement.

Avoid it. Not far from where we live there are some restaurants that specialize in pies. They serve everything from old-fashioned apple pie to some of the most sumptuous chocolate and cream-filled creations that you can imagine. A lot of teenagers visit these pie houses; so do their parents, grandparents, and younger brothers and sisters. If you're on a diet, however, these definitely are not the places to go just to get coffee. The temptations are so strong that few people emerge from these places without having gorged themselves with calories.

Probably you already see how this relates to peer pressure. If you have trouble avoiding temptation (and all of us do), then whenever you can it is wise to avoid situations that tempt you. If some people put you under special pressure, then it is best to steer clear of contacts with such people lest you become like them.

Confess it.   Let's suppose, however, that you fall and do something you know is wrong. Is there any hope for you?

The answer is a strong YES. The Bible couldn't be clearer: "If we confess our sins to him [Jesus Christ], he can be depended on to forgive us and to cleanse us from every wrong" (1 John 1:9). God never stops forgiving, and whenever we are forgiven, we can start over—expecting, resisting, counteracting, and avoiding the peer pressures that cause us to fall.

I wish I had known all of this when I was a teenager. If I had, then maybe those years would not have been so unhappy. With God's help, I might have been able to deal better with peer pressure. With God's help *you* can cope with peer stress now, and that will help you to get along better in later life.

4

Chemical Stress: What to Do About Drugs and Alcohol

I've got a friend who knows a lot about drugs. He's a counselor who works for the state and spends his days talking with kids who are heavy users of pot, alcohol, and a lot of other chemicals.

Before I started writing this chapter I called my friend, and we had some long talks about teenagers and drugs. He loaned me a bunch of books, quoted some sobering statistics about drug use, and then told me about some of his teenage friends.

There's Chuck, for example. (That's not his real name.) He is a fifteen-year-old whose mother took him to the police after he got drunk and kicked a hole in the front door of the house. Chuck drinks pretty regularly and smokes about four or five joints of marijuana every week. This annoys his mother (she doesn't drink or smoke), but his parents are even more upset by Chuck's three recent arrests—one for shoplifting, one for breaking and entering, and one for damaging public property. The judge recently gave Chuck a choice between jail or counseling. He chose counseling, but he isn't too keen on the idea and doesn't really want to change.

Marie had no chance to change. Not long ago she went to a party at the home of a friend whose parents were on vacation. Like everyone else, she was drinking and popping pills. I guess nobody saw her fall to the bottom of the swimming pool, but that's where she was discovered the next morning.

In contrast, the police found Hal wandering nude in a field late at night. He didn't know who he was, and the medical report showed that he was confused, covered with cuts and scratches, bleeding at the mouth (where he had lost two teeth), and swollen around his red, bloodshot eyes. For several hours he swung back and forth between deep sleep and periods when he was cooperative and alert. "I smoked some angel dust," he told the doctors later. "I guess I got awfully stoned!"

I could tell you more stories like these. They're interesting and sad, but they're not unusual. Probably you could come up with sad stories of your own. If you're like most teens, you've read about drug abuse and you may have seen some of your friends get hurt when they were high.

I suppose you've also heard some of the statistics that alarm your parents, teachers, and other adults:

At least half a million teens may be alcoholic, and one in every four teenagers age fourteen and under drinks enough to be considered a moderate drinker (says *Read* magazine).

Thirty-three percent of high school students get drunk at least once a month (reports *Seventeen* magazine).

One out of four high schoolers is a moderate to heavy drinker (according to Research Triangle Institute).

Sixty-five percent of high school seniors have used illegal

drugs at some time in their lives, and one out of four smokes cigarettes regularly (according to research done by the University of Michigan).

Someplace I read that 4,000 teenagers will be killed and 40,000 will be injured this year because of drunk driving.

It's easy to take all of this for granted. Statistics about other people don't mean much to most of us, and if psychologists have learned one thing for sure it is this: People don't avoid drugs or stop taking them just because they hear a few horror stories or read some statistics. The drug problem isn't that simple. So let's try to answer some questions that you probably have been wanting to ask.

Why Do Teens Use Drugs?

There is no reason to explain here why people drink or take other drugs. Of course, most of us take aspirin for headaches, cold and flu tablets when we're not feeling well, and prescription drugs when the doctor says we need them. That kind of drug isn't what we are talking about here. Neither are we greatly concerned about the caffeine which we find in coffee, tea, or cola drinks such as Coke, Tab, or Pepsi.

The kinds of drugs that really create problems are those which are used to "calm you down" or to "turn you on"; those drugs which you can't walk into a store and buy.

Most of these drugs are listed in the chart on the next two pages. Even though it was prepared by the National Institute on Drug Abuse, I almost didn't include it in this book because at first it looks so complicated.

But it isn't!

If you look at it for a minute you will see that the information in these eight columns might be very useful for you. Column 1 gives you the official drug names, while column 2 gives the names most often used. Column 7 is especially interesting because it tells how people are affected by overdoses. Most people

Common Drugs of Abuse

	1	2	3	4 Dependence	
CATEGORY	Drugs	Sample trade or other names	Medical uses	Physical	Psychological
CANNABIS	Marijuana	Pot, grass, reefer, sinsemilla	Under investigation	Unknown	Moderate
	Tetrahydrocannabinol	THC			
	Hashish	Hash	None		
	Hash oil	Hash oil			
DEPRESSANTS	Alcohol	Liquor, beer, wine	None	High	High
	Barbiturates	Secobarbital, Amobarbital, Butisol, Tuinal	Anesthetic, anti-convulsant, sedative, hypnotic	High-moderate	High-moderate
	Methaqualone	Quaalude, Sopor, Parest	Sedative, hypnotic	High	High
	Tranquilizers	Valium, Librium, Equanil, Miltown	Anti-anxiety, anti-convulsant, sedative	Moderate to low	Moderate
STIMULANTS	Cocaine	Coke, flake, snow	Local anesthetic	Possible	High
	Amphetamines	Biphetamine, Dexedrine	Hyperactivity, narcolepsy		
	Nicotine	Tobacco, cigars, cigarettes	None	High	High
	Caffeine	Coffee, tea, cola drinks, No-Doz		Low	Low
HALLUCINOGENS	LSD	Acid	None	None	Degree unknown
	Mescaline and peyote	Button, Cactus			
	Phencyclidine	PCP, angel dust	Veterinary anesthetic	Unknown	High
	Psilocybin - psilocin	Mushrooms	None	None	Degree unknown
INHALANTS	Nitrous oxide	Whippets, laughing gas	Anesthetic	Possible	Moderate
	Butyl nitrite	Locker Room, Rush	None		
	Amyl nitrite	Poppers, snappers	Heart stimulant		
	Chlorohydrocarbons	Aerosol paint, cleaning fluid	None		
	Hydrocarbons	Aerosol propellants gasoline, glue, paint thinner	None		
NARCOTICS	Opium	Paregoric	Antidiarrheal, pain relief	High	High
	Morphine	Morphine, Pectoral Syrup	Pain relief, cough medicine		
	Codeine	Codeine, Empirin Compound with Codeine, Robitussin A-C		Moderate	Moderate
	Heroin	Horse, smack	Under investigation	High	High
	Methadone	Dolophine, Methadose	Heroin substitute, pain relief		

5	**6**	**7**	**8**
Effects in hours	**Possible effects**	**Effects of overdose**	**Withdrawal symptoms**
2-4	Euphoria, relaxed inhibitions, increase in heart and pulse rate, reddening of the eyes, increased appetite, disoriented behavior	Anxiety, paranoia, loss of concentration, slower movements, time distortion	Insomnia, hyperactivity, and decreased appetite occasionally reported
1-12	Slurred speech, disorientation, drunken behavior	Shallow respiration, cold and clammy skin, dilated pupils, weak and rapid pulse, coma, possible death	Anxiety, insomnia, tremors, delirium, convulsions, possible death
1-16			
4-8			
½-2	Increased alertness, excitation, euphoria, increase in pulse rate and blood pressure, insomnia, loss of appetite	Agitation, increase in body temperature, hallucinations, convulsions, possible death, tremors	Apathy, long periods of sleep, irritability, depression
2-4		Agitation, increase in pulse rate and blood pressure, loss of appetite, insomnia	
8-12	Illusions and hallucinations, poor perception of time and distance	Drug effects becoming longer and more intense, psychosis	Withdrawal symptoms not reported
Variable			
6			
Up to ½ hr.	Excitement, euphoria, giddiness, loss of inhibitions, aggressiveness, delusions, depression, drowsiness, headache, nausea	Loss of memory, confusion, unsteady gait, erratic heart beat and pulse, possible death	Insomnia, decreased appetite, depression, irritability, headache
3-6	Euphoria, drowsiness, respiratory depression, constricted pupils, nausea	Slow and shallow breathing, clammy skin, convulsions, coma, possible death	Watery eyes, runny nose, yawning, loss of appetite, irritability, tremors, panic, chills and sweating, cramps, nausea
12-24			

who take an overdose don't intend to do so, of course, but once they get started with a drug, it is hard to stop. Sometimes the results are disastrous—even fatal.

Believe it or not, a lot of kids start taking these kinds of drugs because of the *example of their parents*. Not long ago a cartoon appeared in the *Wall Street Journal*. Sitting at the bar, a distressed looking teen is telling the bartender, "I'm trying to solve my problems like an adult." I smiled when that cartoon first appeared, but it really is more tragic than funny. It's also true.

If your parents drink a lot or take other drugs, you might have decided—unlike the guy in the cartoon—that you won't do the same. It has been found, however, that between 40 and 60 percent of the children of alcoholics become heavy drinkers themselves. This doesn't have to happen, of course—it really depends on you—but when stresses build up in your life there is a tendency to handle pressures the way your parents did. If they tried to cope by using drugs or by drinking, you could find yourself doing the same thing.

Pressure from other teens is an even more common reason for teenage drug use. Just to see if peer pressure really is important, some university scientists recently surveyed almost 17,000 high school seniors and asked them about their use of drugs. As expected, most teens who had tried drugs did so for the first time because of urgings from their friends. Then, once a person started using drugs regularly, he or she was likely to introduce others to the experience. As you would guess, teenage drug users also tend to stick together, often getting high with their friends.

One thing is almost certain. Unless you live and go to school in a very unusual place, sooner or later you will have to make some decisions about drug use (and that includes alcohol). Drugs are all around us, and they are not really difficult to get. Some of your friends use them regularly and may be enthusiastic about inviting others, like you, to get involved. To say no is risky, because your friends might criticize and put you down. If you've never taken drugs, you're probably curious about what it is like to get high or drunk, and since you only plan to try it "just once" it is easy to give in. If the first experience is really good, giving in the next time is easier.

Several years ago (and in some places today) glue sniffing was a popular pastime among high schoolers. Usually airplane glue or some other kind of plastic cement would be squeezed into a bag, and then the fumes would be inhaled into the lungs. The result was often a feeling of silliness and dizzy excitement.

At a party following a high school play, a friend of mine was urged to go into the basement of the home where a large group of the kids had gathered. To his surprise, he found about a dozen of his friends sitting on the floor sniffing glue, and they invited him to join the circle. In his mind, my friend knew that he should say no, but it was hard to resist.

Then he thought of a good way out. Why not hold the bag over his nose, but breathe through his mouth? His friends would never know, especially since most of them were high anyway.

At first this seemed like a good idea, but then my friend decided to take a little sniff or two just to see what it was like.

He remembers the light-headed feeling and the decision to sniff again, but he can't remember leaving the house, wandering out into the street (where the police picked him up), and being admitted to a hospital where he later woke up, looking into the eyes of his anxious parents. After a few days he recovered and went back to school, but his brain has been damaged just enough to dull his thinking and to take the sharpness from his mind.

We all know that things like this don't happen to everyone. Some kids get drunk or high once or twice, recover completely, and never use drugs again. For others, the first sniff, pill, or sip begins a long slide into addiction—a slide that nobody predicted and nobody wanted, but which began because of the urgings of well-meaning friends.

We can't blame all drug abuse on friends, however. Some experts think that a more important cause of drug use is the *buildup of stress*. Apparently, some people start using drugs because this gives them a temporary escape from the pressures of life.

Long before you picked up this book, you knew that most teens (like most of their parents and teachers) are bothered at times with disappointment, guilt, boredom, loneliness, worry, the fear of failure, criticism, and many other problems. There is no fun in sitting around feeling miserable, so if we can't find a sympathetic friend to help us, we often turn to some chemical that will make us feel better. Magazines and television advertisements have told us for years what many of our neighbors believe without question: A drink will help us calm down; popping a few pills will help us forget our troubles.

Sometimes teenagers find that most of their troubles come from parents or other adults who get especially uptight and angry if their kids start playing around with sex or drugs. For some people, therefore, drugs are used as *a form of protest;* a way to get back at others with whom we disagree. It's a technique that works! Parents *do* get upset. But this only makes the existing problems worse, and the protester who takes the drugs is the one who eventually gets hurt the most.

At the root of a lot of drug abuse there exists another cause: *a feeling of inner emptiness.* Many people today, teenagers included, struggle with boredom, religious confusion, uncertainty over what is right or wrong, and a vague feeling that life is meaningless and empty. In a futile effort to fill the emptiness, these people turn to drugs. They don't realize—or they don't *believe*—that only God can permanently fill an inner hole of emptiness. "Don't drink too much . . . ," the Bible states, since many problems lie along this path, "be filled instead with the Holy Spirit, and controlled by him" (Ephesians 5:18). To put it another way, God fills that inner void a lot better than drugs!

What Can You Do About Drugs?

I get sad when I think about Lisa. She's nineteen now and these days is wearing long sleeves. Her right arm shows scars where the needles have been injected countless times, and the left arm is bandaged where she tried to slash her wrist a few days ago.

When she was thirteen, Lisa started drinking and soon moved on to cocaine and PCP. She dropped out of school after ninth grade and hasn't been able to hold a job. She has been arrested about a dozen times on charges ranging from driving without a license to robbery, prostitution, and something called aggravated battery. Lisa has tried a variety of drugs including heroin (which she doesn't like) and whiskey. Her counselor learned that Lisa drinks about twelve beers and takes seven to ten valiums every day, and she uses cocaine on weekends. She would like to make something of herself, but she doesn't have much hope. That's why she tried suicide. If she had cut a little deeper, her drug problems might have been over by now.

But there are better ways to deal with drug problems—and the sooner you think about this, the better.

First, use your brain to think about all of this. It's not likely that you will avoid or stop using drugs just because some author like me encourages you to keep your body free of harmful chemicals. Unless we have met personally, you don't even know me, so why should you take advice from a stranger?

Most likely you'll agree, however, that it does make sense to get facts about drugs. Accurate facts are found in up-to-date encyclopedias (these, of course, are in every library) or in books written by people who really know what they are talking about. For example, you might want to look at a book entitled *Drug Abuse: What Can We Do?* It is clearly written and easy to understand. It is published by Regal Books (Ventura, California). The author, Loyd V. Allen, Jr., is a professor of pharmaceutics at the University of Oklahoma College of Pharmacy.

With all respect, I must admit that parents and other adults sometimes get emotional about these issues, and their facts may not be much more accurate than the conclusions of your drug-using friends. Often, other people have strong opinions about drugs, but they may be short on solid facts, and unless they have studied this carefully they rarely understand the long-term effects of harmful drugs.

Even when they know the facts, however, people often overlook them and use drugs anyway. Medical research has shown, for example, that cigarette smoking is harmful to your health, but many doctors and nurses ignore all of this and smoke like chimneys. (If you don't believe this, ask anyone who eats regularly in a hospital cafeteria.) Apparently knowing about the dangers of drugs does not always stop us from using them.

To prevent addiction, then, we also must learn to deal with the issues that cause us to drink or to use drugs in the first place.

If you are like the kid in that cartoon who is trying to solve problems by drinking because that is what adults do, then try to find better ways to handle stress. If your parents often use drugs and alcohol, think about whether you really want to be like them. This whole book is written to help you cope with life's pressures. Facing such problems squarely lets you rise above them before they get bigger. Using drugs to dull your stresses only hides them, and then you're not alert enough to see that when problems are ignored, they tend to get worse. Many of the teens I know are waking up to the fact that chemicals are not the best way to get relief when stresses arise. More and more adults should be reaching the same conclusions.

But how do you handle the pressure that comes from your friends? Since most drug use begins as a result of peer pressure, it makes sense to think about what you will do the next time some friend invites you to have a drink or offers you drugs. It helps if you make up your mind *now* to say no. Look over the suggestions for handling peer pressure in chapter 3, and when you get to chapter 7, think about drugs again. When we learn to accept and like ourselves (that is what chapter 7 is about), we do not have to depend so much on the approval of others. It is harder to say no and easier to get into drugs when our whole lives swirl around the question of whether or not other people accept us. Of course, their approval is important, but in time most of them respect us even more when they see that we have the courage to stand up for our convictions.

I discovered this when I joined the Canadian reserve navy at eighteen and went off for basic training. The days were long, the training was difficult, and the recruits soon learned that it was important to stick together. Sticking together usually meant drinking, and the alcohol flowed so freely sometimes that it almost seemed to be a part of the boot camp experience. I was over a thousand miles away from home, living with some great people who didn't really know me or my beliefs, who didn't care about my church background, and who would never tell my mother if I got drunk. As you can imagine, the peer pressure was intense, but without putting down anybody else, I decided to say "No, thanks" when I was encouraged to drink. At first I got some criticism, but later I found both acceptance and admiration because I had not gone along with the crowd. At times I was lonely (especially when everyone else was out drinking), but inside I felt good about myself. At the end of one training period, some of my friends even asked if I would help them clean up their language so they wouldn't slip and say something filthy around the family dinner table when they went back home. They had seen I was different because I had not gone along with the crowd, and they respected that.

I must admit that in all of this, my religion helped, just as it has helped others. Several years ago some psychologists took a survey of over five thousand students and discovered that churchgoers are the least likely to take drugs. Drug abuse was most common among the people who ignore God completely.

This doesn't mean that churchgoers never take drugs. Many do. It also doesn't mean that if you go to church you will find some magic way to get off drugs.

What we do know is that Jesus Christ gives help and peace to all who are willing to let Him be in control of their lives. Even if you don't know much about prayer, you can talk to Him. You can expect that He will help you to resist harmful peer pressure, to cope better with life's problems, and to keep away from drugs.

Sometimes a friend can help too. If you are involved in drug use or even are tempted in that direction, think of someone who could give you encouragement and counseling. Teachers, church leaders, parents, neighbors, youth leaders, school counselors—most would be willing to help, and they could get you to a professional counselor if you need one. To admit a problem and to work on it is a healthy sign. It certainly beats suicide (which was Lisa's decision), and it keeps you from becoming a statistic like those mentioned earlier.

How Can You Help Drug Users?

Before we end this chapter, perhaps we should say something about the teenager who is not so much concerned about taking drugs as with helping someone else who has a drug problem. Literally millions of kids in this country have friends who are on drugs, and a huge number live in a home where one or both parents is alcoholic.

Most people hope that if they wait long enough, the other person's drug problem will go away by itself. That seldom happens! If a relative or someone you love is consistently high or drunk, then let me suggest that you consider the following ideas:

Admit to yourself that there is a problem which isn't getting better.

Talk to somebody about your fears, your feelings, and ways in which your friend might be able to get help. You could start by talking with a pastor, a school counselor, or a trusted friend. If your friend or parent is on alcohol, write to Al-Anon Family Group Headquarters (P.O. Box 182, Madison Square Station, New York, N.Y. 10159) or to the National Council on Alcoholism (733 Third Avenue, New York, N.Y. 10017) and ask them what to do. Teenagers with alcoholic parents often meet in Alateen groups. Look in the telephone book for the Alcoholics

Anonymous number and call to see if an Alateen group meets near you.

Recognize that you probably won't have much success trying to reason or argue with your friend, especially if he or she is high or drunk.

Try to remain a friend who cares, but don't cover up for someone else's actions while he or she is drunk or high. Remember that by yourself you probably won't be able to rescue the drug user from his or her problems. The problems and their solutions are not your sole responsibility. Even professional counselors often find it difficult to help a drug user.

So decide to pray, and do so regularly. According to the Bible, earnest prayer "has great power and wonderful results" (James 5:16)—even with people who have problems with drugs and alcohol.

5

Parent Stress:
Crossing the Generation Gap

Jay Kesler has a lot of contact with teenagers. In addition to being the father of teenage kids, he is president of Youth for Christ in the United States and has traveled all over the world speaking to teens and older people who work full-time in youth programs.

In talking with teens about their parents, Jay Kesler has discovered that there are five complaints which come up again and again:

"My parents don't trust me."

"My parents don't love me."

"My parents don't listen to me."

"My parents pick on me."

"My parents are hypocrites."

Not long ago when I asked a large group of teens to list the stresses that bothered them most, almost 80 percent put "getting along with parents" near the top of the list. Some of these teens complained that parents were too busy to spend time with them, others felt that parents didn't try to understand or communicate, and some were frustrated because parents "give us rules but don't say why we need them." Even if your parents are loving and understanding, there probably are times when you have hassles at home.

What can you do about parent stress? You might not find that all of the following suggestions are helpful, but maybe some can help you to get along better. These suggestions are not listed in any special order of importance, but it probably is best to begin with some thoughts about the way in which parents might look at their conflicts with you.

Most Parents Are Not Sure How to Handle Teens

I read once that although many parents feel confused, scared, and inexperienced in dealing with teens, most are loving and really sincere in their desire to get along in the home. As a parent of teenagers, I think this is a pretty accurate description of me and of our friends who are parents.

We are *confused* because we don't always know how to talk with you. We have forgotten what it is like to be a teenager, and sometimes we don't understand your attitudes, moods, feelings, taste in music, beliefs, and standards of right and wrong. Some parents have forgotten that you have powerful sexual urges, strong pressure from your peers, and a sincere desire for independence—except when it comes time for bills to be paid. A lot of parents fail to realize that the world has changed during the past fifteen to thirty years. Teens today have pressures that are different and probably greater than what your parents faced in the "good old days" before you were born. All parents have been teenagers, of course, but that was long ago and it is easy for us to misunderstand your struggles and to forget your desire to be understood and treated with respect.

We don't like to admit it, but some of us are also *scared*—or at least a bit nervous. You are now moving out on your own and that's good. But we've read about teenage alcoholism, about kids who get involved in cults or crime, about the number of teens who smoke pot, and about teenage sex and pregnancies. Even parents who trust their kids wonder if they will get involved with bad company or make tragic mistakes which could have life-shattering effects. Many parents are also scared about how you will turn out, and some are worried about how your actions will reflect on the family. And what if you decide to reject your parents? That might give you a real sense of freedom, but it can be devastating for mothers and dads whose whole adult lives have been spent watching over you. To risk losing your kids is scary.

Also, most of us are *inexperienced*. When my oldest daughter turned thirteen, we had a little discussion after the birthday celebration (I tried not to make it a lecture): "You've never been a teenager before," I said, stating the obvious, "but then, I've never been the parent of a teenager—so we'll have to learn together." I confess that I've made some mistakes and I know I'll make some more. It helps everybody, however, when parents can admit that they are uncertain about what to do and floundering because of their inexperience.

Do you think most parents are *loving?* According to Jay Kesler, a lot of teens would answer no. I wonder, however, if parents and teenagers really do love each other but fail to communicate this very well. Sometimes parents say, "I love you" in the strangest ways: by spending their hard-earned money on vacations, food, allowances, and skating lessons; by letting you keep a dog when they really don't like the inconvenience of animals; by driving you around like a chauffeur before you get your license and, later, letting you drive the family car; by asking questions that really express their concern, but which sometimes seem like prying; and by urging you to study or clean your room, not because they want to "bug" you, but because they are trying to help you learn responsibility (and keep half-eaten sandwiches from rotting under the debris).

It is good to say "I love you" in all of these ways, but it seems to me that parents also should say "I love you" in words, by showing you respect, and by making themselves available to you. It shouldn't surprise you to read, however, that parents like to hear some words of love, respect, and encouragement from you, too.

Not long ago we were on a family trip, and my wife went into a travel office to get some brochures. As she walked back to where we were waiting in the car one of the kids said, "Look at her, Dad. She's really a pretty good mother!" When my wife heard about this remark later, she was in a state of jubilation for three weeks. It is amazing how parents respond to sincere appreciation.

This is partially because most of us really want to be good parents. For every book written to help teenagers get along with parents (I only know of about three), there are a dozen books written for parents. These are best-sellers. Most parents want to get along with you as much as or more than you want peace with them. Of course, we all make mistakes, but when everyone tries to get along, homelife becomes a lot less stressful.

Parents Have Problems Too

All human beings tend to think that their problems are worse than those of other people. Caught up in the stresses of being a teenager, you may not have thought much about the fact that parents have their own problems and pressures. When they don't have (or make) time to be with the family or when they seem especially irritable, the reasons may have little to do with you.

With a few different examples, this book could have been

written for parents instead of for teens. Like you, most parents feel pressure—from their peers, from the people at work, from family members, and sometimes even from their own parents. Some of your parents have poor self-images and great feelings of inferiority. Many don't know how to get along with people, and most grapple at times with feelings of discouragement, fear, and frustration. They might not mention this to you, but many adults are bothered by financial pressures (with a bigger income, financial problems often get larger), religious questions, decisions about work, and the power of sexual temptations or frustrations. Unlike you, parents may also have marital tensions, concerns about aging relatives, and worries about you and your brothers and sisters. For you, the future is bright and filled with hope. For parents, there is a vague awareness that life is "moving right along," that age is creeping up, and that opportunities are fading.

I'm not trying to give you a sob story. When teenagers complain that parents don't understand them, the complaint is probably true. But do *you* understand your parents? When kids try to understand adult problems, parents are often very grateful even if they don't say so at first. This understanding can reduce some of the tensions at home, and it may even help your parents to be more understanding of you.

Several years ago our family moved to Switzerland so I could write a book about an old counselor and writer named Paul Tournier. He is one of those grandfatherly people who radiates warmth, understanding, and love for people—especially teenagers. One day he made this interesting comment: "We old folks should really get along well with young people because we've got the same problems—like lack of money, confusion about the future, and changes within our bodies." I think the wise doctor has made an interesting point. If all of us could recognize and try to understand the problems of older—and younger—people, we'd move a long way toward reducing war and maintaining peace in the home.

Honesty Is a Good Policy

Parents and teachers sometimes forget that teenagers are between two worlds but not quite a part of either. You certainly are not children who need to be pampered, minded, and protected. Some of you have your own jobs, drive your own cars, and make many of your own decisions. But even if you are six feet tall, society still does not call you an adult. You can't vote until you are eighteen. You have only limited control over your circumstances, especially if you depend on others for shelter, education, and most of your money, food, and clothes. Many older people treat you as an "adultlet," who wants the freedom but doesn't have the money, age, or opportunities to take on full adult responsibilities.

Parents have a great tendency to forget that you are between these two worlds. Sometimes we treat you like babies, reminding you to wear a sweater when it's cold and telling you how to behave in church. Our sincere concern for you at times gets close to nagging. At other times we may give you more responsibility than you can handle and then gripe because you don't always act like adults.

Maybe there are times when parents need a reminder of where you are. This happened in our house on the day I wrote these words. Our daughter Lynn came to the breakfast table looking tired and clearly not ready to leave for school. Without thinking, I started to "hurry her up," but soon I was caught short.

"Don't be so impatient, Dad," her sister Jan suggested gently. "Lynn really *is* almost ready and she will be able to leave on time. She usually does."

As a father, I don't really know what is involved in getting a female teenager ready for school, and I appreciated Jan's suggestion that I "cool it" with my criticisms.

Perhaps I also appreciated the reminder because of the way it was done. Parents don't like cutting, sarcastic put-downs any more than teens do. But when a teen points things out in a way that is polite, respectful, and kind, parents feel less threatened and are more likely to respond without a fight. This is important to remember if you want to point something out to your parents, or if you think they are not being completely honest. At the start of this chapter I mentioned that many kids think their parents are hypocrites. According to my big, fat dictionary, hypocrites are people who pretend to be one way, but whose actions show that they are something different.

Ted was a former student of mine whose father was a leader in the local church. He served on many church committees and was praised as a super Christian. At home, however, Ted's dad was violent. He beat his family, yelled, criticized, and sometimes would explode in anger on his way to or from the church where everybody thought that he was so pious and spiritual. I never saw Ted's dad at home (I know him only as a church leader), but if Ted's description was correct, the man clearly was a hypocrite.

Ted could have argued with his dad, or tried to overlook the mean actions at home. Instead, Ted looked at himself to make sure he wasn't a hypocrite as well. (Remember, Jesus once said it is important that you take care of your own faults before you start criticizing others.) Then Ted decided to honestly point out his father's inconsistencies. It was done slowly, respectfully, and with gentleness. Ted had learned that people get angry or feel threatened if you list their failures or weaknesses too abruptly.

Instead, it is better to say some nice things about people, along with the criticisms. Instead of accusing and making comments that condemn and get people mad, start your critcisms with phrases like these:

"You know, I've noticed something lately which has bothered me . . ."

"I feel bad about something, and it would help me if we could discuss it . . ."

"I wonder if you've got the time to let me run something by you which is concerning me . . ."

Use your own words, of course, try to keep from shouting, and avoid such emotional words as *you always* or *you never*. Expect that your parents might not always respond favorably even to such gentle, honest conversation. It is possible that your suggestions will scare them to death, since many have never tried to handle problems in this straightforward way. If you give them time to respond, however, most will come to appreciate the honesty and peace that can follow.

But be prepared for the fact that some parents never change. Ted's dad didn't, so the son learned to put up with the tirades at home. Ted also has learned to accept the fact that, like teens, adults are different from one another. Your parents are not like all other adults. As you are aware, some people outside the home are easier to get along with than your parents; others are not.

Explosions Rarely Accomplish Anything

I know some counselors who believe that when people are angry they should be encouraged to yell and argue since this lets off steam and reduces tension for a while.

That may be true (if you emphasize *for a while*), but hollering and fighting do not help to really solve anything, and often such explosions create more problems—like hurt feelings, discouragement, misunderstanding, and a lot of frustration. Of course, when you have a disagreement it isn't easy to speak gently and think clearly, but the words of Solomon which we quoted in a previous chapter apply equally well at home. "A soft answer turns away wrath, but harsh words cause quarrels" (Proverbs 15:1).

It is always helpful to remember the obvious—quarrels have two sides. When tension starts to build, ask yourself, *What might I be doing that's making things worse? What could I do to calm things down? Are there some things that I can overlook?*

You know about garbage collectors, but have you ever heard of *grievance collectors* (I mentioned them in chapter 1)? You probably know some of these people. You may have some who are relatives, and it is possible that you might be one yourself. Grievance collectors are always looking for bad habits or actions in other people that are annoying. Occasionally someone will write down a list of these annoyances, but usually we tuck them into our minds waiting for the next fight. Then when we have a disagreement we bring out all of the ammunition that we have stockpiled in preparation for war.

Grievance collectors are really unhappy people. Their lives are spent searching for complaints they can hurl at others or use as the basis for nagging. Isn't it better to overlook some things and to search for the positive in others? The Bible writers who told us to encourage and build up one another knew how to make peace in the home. Isn't it tragic that so many people try to get along by building up themselves and putting down one another by hurling complaints and grievances? This never works to remove stress from the home.

Trust Is Something to Be Earned

What do you do if your parents don't trust you?

If you are like most people you are likely to feel hurt, put down, and perhaps angry because this lack of trust may seem so unfair. It helps to remember that your parents are probably concerned about your happiness. They don't want you to fall into situations where you could be hurt physically or harmed in other ways. Very often, however, this parental concern seems to border on too much control, and that can be frustrating to say the least.

The place to begin with this problem is to let your parents see that you can be trusted. *Do* try to cooperate, get home on time, get up when called, drive carefully, let them know where you are, take responsibility for your schoolwork or jobs around the house, and be diligent in your music practice or athletic involvement. *Do not* sneak out, ignore or deliberately break their rules, disrespect their opinions, or refuse to admit your mistakes. Do whatever you can to communicate the message "I can be trusted." If they see that you are responsible, they are more likely to trust you.

But I know some parents who never get the message. They specialize in emphasizing what is wrong about you and overlook the good things. When parents miss the point, tell them. Try not to be argumentative (that only creates conflict), but show them evidence that says you can be trusted. Then back up your words with actions. Just as we don't need parental hypocrites, we don't need teen hypocrites either—pretenders who say one thing and do something different.

Learn to Listen and Communicate

We've mentioned this before, but it is worth bringing up again. A lot of teens complain that their parents don't listen, and it may surprise you to learn that a lack of communication is one of the major causes of family breakups.

In studying to become a psychologist, I learned that listening takes time and energy. It also takes a strong desire to really know what others are thinking and trying to communicate. Do you really want to be understood and to understand others (the two go together)? If so, always try to state your views clearly and, above all, take time to listen.

Sometimes we get the idea that we can set aside special times for communicating and growl at each other for the rest of the week. That doesn't work. There can be real value in setting aside some time for talking, but to really get along we must be ready to listen and talk *whenever* the need or opportunity arises. In our family, some of the best communication takes place without warning when we are painting a room, driving someplace in the car, or stopping someplace for ice cream. If your parents never are involved in such informal activities, invite them to come with you.

Then, sometime when you are talking, bring up the issue of parental rules. Be careful not to set up a fight, but when rules seem unreasonable you might try an approach like this:

"Dad, I'm going to do what you say, but you must have some reason for this, and it would help if I could understand," or, "I'm struggling with this and it would help if you could share with me why this is important."

If reasons are given, listen and try to understand instead of doing what comes naturally to all of us: finding arguments to defend your position.

Some Things Never Change

Even when you try hard to communicate and get along, you may discover that things don't get much better. Some family tensions persist in spite of what you do. Some parents will never seem to change, especially in response to your suggestions. You may do everything possible to get along but discover that the wars at home still keep on being fought. When this happens, remember two things.

First, you won't be there forever. It may take a lot of patience for you to survive, but within a few years you'll be on your own.

I know a lady who grew up in France during the Nazi occupation. There was no fuel for heating and little to eat except a few crusts of bread and weeds. Times were difficult, but the family held on because they knew that things would get better sooner or later.

The same is true with you. Living at home may be tough (even if they don't expect you to eat weeds), but the end is not too far away.

While you are waiting, learn from your parents. That's my second suggestion. It is sobering to realize that most kids grow up to be a lot like their parents. Will you?

When I was in my late teens, in the reserve navy, some of our experiences in boot camp were pretty tough, especially when some of the officers picked on the recruits. One of these was a frustrated little guy named Midshipman Lee. Whenever he was criticized, his response was "I'll be kind if I ever get to be an officer." I don't know if Lee ever became a navy lieutenant, but if he did, I hope he learned from the miseries of being in boot camp. I hope he didn't turn out to be a sadist like some of those officers.

You can learn from watching your parents. Can you pick up their good qualities and make sure you don't take on those traits that aren't so good? Being a teenager is like being in a boot camp preparing for adulthood. What you learn now can make you a better person in the future. Someday *you* might be a parent of teenagers. If you can learn now how to get along, your teenagers will be grateful in the future, and life in your house will be a lot less stressful.

God Can Help You Get Along With Your Parents

I've never met Tim Stafford, but I've read his articles in *Campus Life* and know that he really understands teens. Recently, in a book called *The Trouble with Parents*, he wrote some powerful words about God and your family.

> You cannot make your parents change. . . . But what you can't do, God can. If problems with your parents do nothing more than make you start talking to Him regularly, something good has already happened. The simple act of talking to God each day about your family situation may do more good than confrontations, family councils, counselors, and letters written at night.

God can help you to keep cool when the pressures get hot and you want to explode. He knows about the tensions you face. He can help you keep calm and lead you to friends who can encourage you and pray with you.

God can help you to communicate—to say the right words, to understand, to have patience when there is conflict, stubbornness, and confusion.

God can help you to learn. Did you know that many of the children and teens who are beaten and yelled at later treat their own kids in the same way? Parents' mistakes get passed on to the children, so hassling continues generation after generation. But God can help you to be more loving, cooperative, respectful, and a peacemaker at home.

God also can help you to accept things that never change. He doesn't treat people like robots who are programmed to change whether they want to or not. God works in people's minds to help them see things differently, but individual family members must choose to change. Many times no change comes, so God uses the family tension to teach you patience and reliance on Him.

I don't think God likes family conflict. He hates the sin, insensitivity, self-centeredness, impatience, and fighting that so often occurs in the home. When these things persist, however, He uses them to teach willing people how to grow and mature.

What can you learn from the stresses in your home as a result of these pressures? How can you be a different person both now and in the future? Maybe you can think of some practical answers to these questions. You might also ask your parents to read this chapter. Could it be helpful to them?

6

Family Stress: Getting Along When Your Family Falls Apart

A couple of years ago my cousin Glyn died.

He was a successful lawyer, well-known in the city where he lived, and liked by the people who knew him. Unlike some other parents I know, Glyn was interested in his family. He tried hard to be a good father, and his sudden death shocked everyone—especially his wife and three teenage kids.

Not long ago I talked to Glyn's widow. She didn't say much about how the kids were adjusting, but I know it's been hard, like it is with any family that breaks up.

In one sense Glyn's family hasn't broken up. The three teen-agers and their mother still live together and get along—but the father is missing and that hurts. It always hurts when a father dies, or a mother, or one of the kids. It can even hurt when a pet dies. Part of the family has been lost.

But death isn't the only cause of family stress. I know a home where the mother had a serious stroke. She has been unconscious for weeks and probably will never get better. She's not dead. The family members still visit her and pray for her recovery. But she's gone from the home, maybe forever. Somehow the family has to carry on without her, and the uncertainty about her health keeps everybody tense.

Then there are the thousands of families that are split by arguments, the excessive busyness of a father or mother, the criminal activities of a family member, someone's alcoholism, or the parents' decision to separate, divorce, and sometimes to remarry—often without consulting you or without (it seems) even considering your feelings.

If your family is without major tensions like these, then be very thankful. This chapter can let you understand and help other people whose families are not as stable or as happy as the family in your home.

On the other hand, if your family is tense or has been divided by death, divorce, or other painful happenings, then read on. The following paragraphs are especially for you. We'll begin with an important question which is very difficult to answer.

Why Do Families Have Problems?

Probably most of us wonder at times why our families have problems getting along. To find answers, large groups of sociologists, psychologists, teachers, church leaders, authors, newspaper writers, and even a few politicians have analyzed the modern family. They have tried to discover why marriages are so unstable and divorce is so common, why mate beating and child abuse are increasing, and why many families seem to be involved in constant bickering and arguing. Several answers keep popping up whenever these questions are discussed.

First, many problems come because we have learned to be self-centered. For many people, this me-first way of thinking starts at home, but it also is seen in school, in magazine articles, and sometimes even in church. The self-centered view says, "I want my rights and comfort. I expect to get my fair share—even if I have to fight for it. If I don't take care of myself, others will walk all over me." Such thinking causes us to shove and fight as we go through life and, as we all know, a lot of the fighting occurs at home. Instead of trying to build up, encourage, and care for one another (which is what the Bible tells us to do), we criticize, put down, and find fault with each other. Often we don't intend to be mean but we are. We don't think that our words really are self-centered, but they can be. When we lose our tempers, we may refuse to apologize and sometimes even find excuses in our own minds to explain away our actions. I'd hate to tell you how often I've said something unkind at home and then blamed it on the fact that I was tired or under pressure. Even our excuses tend to be self-centered.

This self-centered thinking is closely tied to a second cause of family tension. Many homes have problems because people haven't learned how to communicate. Family members don't say what they mean, don't really listen to one another, and don't try to understand the other person's point of view. At times we use loaded questions like "Why do you always_____?" or "When are you going to start_____?" (You fill in the blanks.) These statements get people mad and lead us to say things that hurt. Then there is more tension and misunderstanding.

Family members would have less tension if we would listen carefully, learn to express ourselves clearly, and try not to put down others. We need to remind ourselves that relatives have feelings and frustrations too. They want to be understood.

But even when you work hard at understanding and communicating, family tensions may still appear. This is because problems rarely come from one person alone. Just as it takes two to argue, it takes two to communicate. If you try and the other person doesn't, some tensions will continue. Then, even if a whole family communicates, there is a third cause for conflict: outside influences.

There can be many of these. A family can be thrown into real turmoil when in-laws interfere, somebody loses a job, there is a serious illness in the family, the car quits, the neighbors are unreasonable, or one of the kids gets pregnant or arrested. These stresses are hard to handle and while they pull some families together, they tear apart others.

Differences of opinion also can divide the family. Husbands and wives, for example, sometimes differ in their view about religion, how to spend money, what to watch on television, or how to handle the kids, including you. These disagreements can become the issues that give rise to unending family wars—wars which often are fought because the warriors have not learned to compromise, or are too stubborn to change.

I once counseled a married couple who argued all the time and often pulled their teenage children into the battles. Before long I concluded that for these people fighting had become a way of life. They didn't know how to relate to each other in any other way, and I don't think they had much interest in changing.

Recently, I read an article about a movie star who had been married for almost twenty-five years. That's unusual, especially in Hollywood, and a newspaper reporter asked how this had happened. "I spend time with the family," the movie star replied. "We try not to fight and we try to keep from getting bored with each other."

At home it is easy to fight, to get bored, or to take each other for granted. It is easy, too, for family members to get so involved with outside activities that home becomes little more than a place to get laundry done and, sometimes, to eat or sleep. When the family members look elsewhere for variety, fun, and companionship, the family eventually breaks up. The relatives may still live together or eat around the same table at Thanksgiving, but people's real interests are elsewhere.

How Can Families Get Along?

We've already mentioned the importance of listening, communicating, and trying to understand each other at home. In addition, many of the ideas we discussed in chapters 2, 3, and 5 apply to homelife in general and can help your family in particular. Of course, all of this takes time and effort, both of which can be so scarce in our busy lives.

Most important, however, is whether or not family members want to get along. When people don't care, nobody tries very hard to build family togetherness. Instead there is tension, conflict, or a tendency for family members to ignore each other and drift apart.

This isn't what God wanted when He created the world and put people in families. He wanted us to respect and care for one another, to show love in our homes, and to give Him a central place in our thinking.

It was only a few years ago when billboards and bumper stickers proclaimed: THE FAMILY THAT PRAYS TOGETHER STAYS TOGETHER. That wasn't just a cute and catchy slogan. It stated something that has been proven by research studies. When compared to others, families that worship God together are less inclined to break up. There can be many reasons for this, but "for starters" praying families turn to God for help and more often try to live in accordance with the Bible's teaching.

It is best when family worship is suggested by one of the parents, but what if your parents aren't interested in praying? What if they don't seem to care much about getting along or communicating with each other and with you? Is it possible for one teenager to bring healing and stability to a tense family?

The answer often is yes. Your influence might not work

quickly, and at times it won't be felt at all. Nevertheless, it is worth trying. Homes can be mended when one teenager tries to:

- be patient, understanding, and respectful;
- communicate clearly;
- pray regularly for the family, asking for God's guidance in dealing with the family problems; and
- encourage family members to get along and to attend church.

Sometimes a trusted counselor or church leader can listen as you talk over your family situation and can make suggestions about other ways in which you can try to help.

What If My Family Breaks Up?

In spite of all these efforts, however, families do break up. In one way this might give you a feeling of relief, especially if there has been a lot of arguing. In other ways, however, a family breakup is very difficult for anyone to handle. It could be one of the most stressful experiences of your teenage years. Let's consider the stress of a separation or divorce first. Later we'll discuss the death of a parent or other family member.

It's not easy to face the fact that your parents might be heading for a divorce. For a while you might not notice the tensions, and later you may try to ignore them. Some teenagers try not to think about the problems at home, or they may convince themselves that things really are getting better instead of worse. Perhaps they try to keep out of the house as much as possible and retreat to their rooms or use loud music to drown out the noise when their parents argue. Often teens tell themselves that there really aren't problems or that they really don't care if their parents can't get along. Sometimes they fail to see that even though parents may not be arguing, they still are growing further and further apart.

At some time you wake up to the fact that your parents are planning to separate. This may or may not come as a surprise but in either case you are likely to be overwhelmed with intense feelings. Anger, sadness, shock, fear about the future, guilt, and a host of other feelings come flooding in to overpower you at the most unexpected times and places. Sometimes you may want to cry, scream, swear, pray, and beg your parents to stay together— all at the same time.

Once you adjust to the shock, you may begin to have a lot of questions. *Where will I live after the separation? Which parent will I stay with? Will I see the other parent? Will we have to move? Will we have financial problems? What will my friends think? Did I cause the breakup?* (You probably didn't.) *How will this affect my brothers and sisters? If my parents remarry, where will I belong?* While you think about these things you may find that your parents are preoccupied with their own problems and less able to take care of your needs or to keep the household running smoothly. Some teenagers find themselves trapped in the middle of a tug-of-war, with each parent trying to get them on their side and lined up against the other parent.

I once knew a girl whose parents separated after their two sons had married and left home. One son sided with the father against the mother; the other son took the mother's side against the father. My friend—we'll call her Angie—loved both parents and both of her brothers, but she watched with horror as the family lined up for battle. Angie's father had left home and gone to live with his girl friend. Since Angie was still in high school, she stayed with her mother, but she was torn between a desire to help her mother, a need to let her father know of her love, and a secret wish to escape from the situation by running off to college. All of this was mixed with guilt, anger, and frustration which lasted well into Angie's adult years.

Maybe the scars will never go away completely, but in time most of the hurt will heal. It helps if you can recognize that your feelings are normal. A school counselor, pastor, older relative, or some other understanding adult might be able to help you sort out your emotions and get a clearer perspective on what is happening. Perhaps you also can learn to understand your parents better, to forgive them, to accept their failures, and even to encourage them. It helps if you have friends who care and can listen sympathetically, but try not to talk about your problems all the time. That can drive people away when you need them most.

Then, accept the fact that your life will be different. There probably will be some loneliness, some confusion, and maybe a change in where and how you live. For a while your grades might slip (it's hard to concentrate when you're hurting and anxious), and you may have trouble getting along with the kids at school. It might hurt to see other families with the parents and children still together. Thanksgiving, Christmas, birthdays, and other celebration times may be especially painful, but remember that you are not the only person in the world who has these stresses. And you aren't an "oddball." Millions of kids live in one-parent families, and after getting adjusted, these families frequently get along fine—sometimes even better than they did when both parents were present, arguing, fighting, or giving one another the "silent treatment." If you think about it, you can even learn from your parents' mistakes and avoid the same problems when you get married.

Right now, however, you should recognize that in many ways the breakup of a family is like death. Your hurt and sorrow are every bit as painful as the grief felt by people whose families are torn apart by death. In both cases it takes time to recover.

What About Death in the Family?

Most of us don't like to think about death, and it's probable that some people will even skip over this section. I'm not sure I blame them. At some time most of us will have to face the death of a parent or other close relative, but we prefer to wait and think about that when the time comes, not now.

But some people are like my cousin's teenagers. Their dad died suddenly and without any prior warning. Other kids may see the end coming, and along with their families, they go through a long and sad waiting period. In either case, it's difficult to cope when death finally arrives.

Each person reacts to death a little differently. You'll probably notice this if you look at yourself and the other members in your family when a death occurs. Some people cry a lot, especially at the beginning. Others hold their feelings inside and pretend it doesn't hurt. At some time, however, most people find that it helps to cry. It's also good to know that it's normal to feel restless, exhausted, anxious, frustrated, bored, irritable, and very sad. You may not feel much like eating, and at times you might feel a big emptiness inside. Nightmares are common, and often you may dream about the person who has died. When you wake up and realize that it was only a dream, you feel a hurting sadness again.

Then there is anger. Some people, maybe you, get mad at God for letting the death occur. Some get mad at themselves because they remember saying something unkind to the person before he or she died. You might even get mad at the person who died, because you have been left to feel so much misery. Of course you realize that such anger is stupid, but it often is there and you might as well admit it.

All of this is describing something called *grief.* It doesn't come just when somebody dies. Grief comes whenever we are separated from someone we love. You can grieve when your parents separate, when your best friend moves away, or when you break up with somebody who has been very special. Even homesickness is a type of grief.

When death comes, however, the separation is more permanent. To squelch your feelings and pretend that they don't exist may seem mature, but in time those pent-up emotions can tear you apart. When you grieve, therefore, don't be afraid to cry (go into a room all by yourself if you don't want to be seen). Talk about your sadness, fears, loneliness, and other frustrations with somebody who is willing to listen. Don't avoid the funeral—that only delays the pain.

Then remember that God, who permitted the death to occur, also loves us, comforts us, and has made it possible for Christians to see their relatives again in heaven. Let God know your feelings (even if you are angry or confused). Ask Him to comfort you and to send people who will love and help you—even when you don't want to be bothered with other human beings.

Almost everybody gets over their grief, but it takes time. You have to accept the fact that life will never be quite like it was before the death took place.

My cousin's picture is in the living room of his house and pinned up on the bulletin board in the kitchen. The family talks freely about their dad and how much they miss him. I suspect they have a hard time at Christmas, vacations, or other holidays when they used to do things together. They'll never completely get over his sudden death—but they are picking up life and going on. That's what their dad would have wanted. That's what God—and their caring friends—are helping them to do.

Stepfamilies

Some families learn to get along pretty well after a divorce has torn them apart or a family member has died. Then, all of a sudden, there is another problem: Your mother (or father) announces plans to get married again.

If you think about this you know that you probably saw it coming. Teenagers are alert enough to know what's going on when their parents start to date. Most of the people who lose a mate early in life get married again—usually without getting permission from their kids.

It's natural for you to have mixed feelings about this. You may feel happiness because your parent is happy, but you might also feel betrayed, forsaken, guilty, resentful, and maybe a little angry. You wonder where *you* fit into this new family. Where will you live? Will your *stepfather* or *stepmother* (even those words seem strange) accept you? Will the new family member bring kids into the marriage, forcing you to share your room or to adjust to stepbrothers or stepsisters whom you don't know and may not like?

It might help you to know that in the United States alone about one child in five lives in a stepfamily. While it isn't easy to adjust, it *is* possible. You may even find that you like your new family.

A lot depends on your attitude. If you complain constantly, refuse to cooperate, and make up your mind that life in the new family will be miserable—it will be. If you honestly discuss your feelings with a friend, minister, school counselor, or parent, you can see things in a clearer perspective. If you try to get along and to be understanding, things are likely to go better.

Popular songs often give us a false idea about love. They imply that we *feel* love first and then *do things* to show our love. True love is exactly the opposite. If we get into the habit of doing kind and loving acts (even when we don't feel like it) we discover that we soon begin to feel positive about others and perhaps even to feel love.

This certainly applies at home. If you can "be nice to others," people often start being nice to you, and real feelings of affection and closeness often follow.

What About Other Family Problems?

Have you noticed that this chapter hasn't mentioned all of the big family problems that teenagers face today?

What do you do, for example, if one of your parents, or a brother or sister, is often drunk? Alcoholism has become a big problem in this country, and whenever it appears, the drinker's family is put under a lot of stress.

Or what about beatings in the home? A lot of husbands and

wives beat up each other, and it appears that many parents physically hurt their kids—including their teenagers. It isn't easy to
live in that kind of a situation.

Then there's the problem that nobody likes to mention—incest. Nobody knows how many fathers lure their daughters into
bed. (It happens between mothers and sons too.) Such teenagers
may feel used, abused, dirty, and guilty—all of these feelings are
common—but often they try to just live with them because they
don't want to hurt the parent. They are afraid of what might
happen if they "squeal," or they feel guilty about betraying the
"little secret" that the parent makes them promise to keep.

To keep quiet, however, will just make matters worse. In one
little chapter there isn't space to deal with serious family problems like this, but you need to discuss them with someone. You
might not feel the need for help, but if you have parents who
can't control themselves (and give way to their drinking, anger,
or sexual urges), then they need help, and the sooner they get it,
the better.

Where do you go for help? Ask yourself who is the wisest and
most concerned adult you know? Try to think of somebody who
won't get "uptight" if you mention such problems. It may be a
relative, teacher, church leader, school counselor, or someone
else. Go to this person in confidence and ask for help as you seek
a solution to your family problem.

Sometimes things won't get any better and they may even get
worse. If you can talk about your family stresses, however, you
can cope better. You can try to find ways to solve the problems.
You can talk to God about them, knowing that He is aware of
the situation and able to work in people's lives to bring change.
That may be the most comforting idea of all.

7

Self Stress:
Learning to Like Yourself

When I was in high school, our English teachers used to assign novels which we were required to read (that was usually enjoyable) and analyze (that I hated). Some of the novelists had a special ability to describe people.

Consider, for example, this paragraph from *The Affair* (Penguin, 1962) by a British writer named C. P. Snow.

> He was a large young man, cushioned with fat, but with heavy bones and muscles underneath. He was already going bald, although he was only in his late twenties. The skin of his face was fine-textured and pink, and his smile was affable, open, malicious, eager to please and smooth with soft soap. As he greeted me, his welcome was genuine, his expression warm: his big bright blue eyes stayed watchful and suspicious.

Good novelists always seem to write like that. They go into a lot of detail describing the physical appearance, abilities, intelligence, and personal traits of the characters in each book.

Now, let us suppose that someone decided to write a story about you. How would they describe you?

Or suppose that *you* were writing a description of yourself. What would you write? (Think about that for a minute.)

If you are like most people, your self-description would include a few good traits listed along with a lot of negative characteristics. Most of us—one expert has suggested 95 percent of the population—see things in ourselves that we don't like. This is true even in people who are oozing with charm, bubbling with self-confidence, and so overstocked with talents, abilities, and good looks that you feel like a cricket in comparison. Most of us are at least a little insecure, and many people have a lot of inferiorities.

Dr. Jim Dobson once suggested that in order to feel good about themselves teenagers in our society need three things: good looks, intelligence, and money.

Let's think first about "looks." According to Dobson, 80 percent of all teenagers are dissatisfied with something about their bodies. Even small flaws create problems because our friends seem to notice and take delight in teasing us about our height, nose, ears, feet, or other parts of the body. Names like "Peewee," "Gorilla," "Duckfeet," "Elephant," and "Miss Piggy" remind people that they are different. Even if we laugh when called such names, it can hurt inside. It also can hurt when people stare but say nothing about the braces on your teeth or the acne that doesn't seem to clear up. You're glad this isn't mentioned, but you wonder what others might be thinking.

Not long ago, as she was leaving school, one of my daughters casually mentioned to a friend that he was "cute" because he was so short. The comment was not said in a nasty way or meant to be unkind, but while everybody laughed I think my daughter's friend must have hurt inside. We learned later that many people comment about this teenager's height, and he is very sensitive about the fact that his growth has been slow.

If anything bothers us as much as our appearance it is the fear that other people might think we are stupid or dumb. Nobody likes to be considered a "lamebrain" or "airhead," and feeling that we aren't very smart can bring forth great feelings of inferiority and self-criticism.

We also can feel inferior when we don't have very much money. In our society, money is one way to measure importance. It is easy to feel unimportant and inferior if you are poor or if you live in a neighborhood and attend a school where everyone else is dressed better, lives in a nicer house, has a better stereo system, or seems to have a lot more cash than you have in your wallet.

If it is true, as Dr. Dobson says, that beauty, brains, and bucks are the most important things for teenagers, then it is likely that most of us will come up short. To make matters worse, other people intentionally or accidentally tend to remind us of our inferiorities.

Think, for example, how devastating it can be when:

- your friends make the honor roll, the basketball team, the cheerleading squad, or the band—but you don't, and everybody knows this;
- you get bad grades, even after trying hard to do better;
- you don't have a date for some big school party—and have no likelihood of getting one;
- the teams are selected in gym class, and you are chosen last; or
- everybody's parents will be at a school game or concert, but yours have decided to stay home.

When these things happen it is not surprising that so many people feel inferior, afraid of failure, foolish, and dissatisfied with themselves.

What can we do about such feelings of inferiority? Let me make several suggestions that might be helpful.

Avoid "Poor-Little-Me" Thinking

It is easy to convince yourself that you are the only one who feels inferior and that you are worse than everybody else. Be careful not to let yourself slip into that kind of thinking! Most people hide their insecurities pretty well, but almost everyone feels inferior about something. You're not some unique, good-for-nothing creature who has to go through life smiling on the outside but inwardly hurting with a "poor-little-me, isn't-it-awful?" attitude.

Perhaps it doesn't help much to know that others feel inferior too. (Misery doesn't always love company.) But it is helpful to realize that you are not an "oddball" just because you feel inferior. It is a common feeling; perhaps the most common personal problem among both teenagers and adults.

Not long ago my kids and I tried out one of those gigantic slides that sometimes appear at state fairs and amusement parks. Although we started down the hill slowly, we soon picked up speed and it didn't take us long to reach bottom.

Some people have a downward slide like this when they feel overwhelmed by their inferiorities. When they think of themselves as being no good or ugly, they don't try to succeed or to get along with people. Since they don't try, they fail. This just convinces them even more that they are no good, so they try even less. Before long they are sliding faster and faster into self-pity, self-hatred, anger, jealousy, more failure, and even greater feelings of self-condemnation.

It's hard to stop yourself when you are sliding into this kind of thinking, but it is possible. Even if you reach bottom, you can always pick yourself up and start the climb back to the top of the hill.

Keep Things in Perspective

When we fail, when something goes wrong, when we are embarrassed, or when we get some disappointing news, it is easy to get discouraged. Maybe that's nature's way of helping us deal with the sad and frustrating events of life.

Often, however, it is so easy to see the dark side of life that we get things out of perspective. Most of the things that make us feel inferior—like a big nose, poor grades, or clumsiness—won't matter much when we are older. Even now, if we think about this for a while, we will see that each of us has a lot of good qualities and abilities which can offset the weaknesses.

Have you ever seen one of those posters that says: GOD DOESN'T MAKE JUNK?

When He made you and me (even with our physical features, feelings, and inborn human nature), He made us the way He wanted. When the human race fell into sin, God sent His son Jesus to take our punishment, because He loves us. He respects us so much that He never forces us to become religious, but as a gift He offers to adopt us as His children. He says, in essence,

> Confess your sins and failures to Me, depend on Me and let Me be Lord of your life and I will make you a part of the family of God. I'll forgive your sins, help you here on earth, promise you eternal life in heaven after you die; and give you some special abilities which you can use to help others. Of course it won't always be easy. Some people will criticize you, others may laugh, and you might even get hurt. But it doesn't matter that much because you are a child of the King of the universe.

When He walked on earth, Jesus kept encountering a group of religious leaders known as the Pharisees. They were holier-than-thou individuals, who constantly compared themselves to others and came out on top. We have a tendency to make comparisons, too, but often we come out on the bottom. Some people even boast about being inferior. This brings several benefits. By saying, "I'm no good," we have an excuse for not trying. Sometimes other people feel uncomfortable or sorry for us when we complain, so they make statements about our fine points and this makes us feel better. But of what value is a compliment that doesn't come freely? Boasting about our inferiorities so someone will deny what we say is not much different from boasting of our greatness.

Wouldn't it be better to think: *God made me like He made everyone else—a valuable person with both strong and weak points. There are some traits or physical features that I wish I had—and others that I would like to get rid of—but there are other things about myself that I do like. I want to build on my strengths instead of moaning and complaining about my weaknesses.* That's keeping things in perspective.

Find Some Friends

Nothing helps get rid of a feeling of inferiority like involvement with others. When we have friends who accept us and care for us, we can be less concerned about our weaknesses and physical features.

But what if you don't have any friends? Let me repeat an old statement that you probably have heard from your grandmother: If you want to have friends, let people know that you are friendly. This doesn't mean forcing yourself on others. Instead it means being considerate, polite, and willing to say "Hi." It means being a listener and not always talking about yourself. Without overdoing it, you also can compliment others, point out their good traits, and pause at times to thank them when they've helped. This makes you more attractive to others, and friendships soon begin to build.

Try to Avoid Self-Defeating Activities

When people feel down because of their inferiorities, they sometimes try to boost themselves by doing and saying things that they think will help but which really make matters worse. Let me give you four examples.

Do you know people who constantly criticize and put down others? Do you know people who are gossips and faultfinders? Usually such people are very insecure. Unconsciously (and sometimes deliberately) they try to make themselves look good by knocking down everyone else. Sometimes such people get bitter, resentful, unforgiving, always thinking about their grudges. They constantly keep beating other people down but eventually they lose because, after a while, nobody pays any attention.

I once knew a professor who was like that. She was a psychologist who believed that her theories were right and everyone else was wrong. At first other people listened, but she was so critical and so unwilling to see anything good in other people that eventually nobody paid much attention to her. I think that's very sad. Down deep she must have felt very insecure and inferior.

A second way people try to hide their inferiorities is to act as if they are successful, capable, and bursting with self-confidence. I'm always a little skeptical when I meet such people. On the outside they seem so fearless and self-assured, but this often is a big front to hide their real feelings of insecurity and fear—like a Halloween mask covers a real face. Such people are great pretenders trying to convince others (and sometimes themselves) that they are different from what they feel inside.

Then, third, there are those who give up in the face of their weaknesses and refuse to try. Sometimes people feel sorry for them, and that gives a little boost to their egos for a while. But who wants to limp through life always telling oneself, *I can't do it*?

One final reaction is to push ourselves so hard in trying to succeed that we ruin our health.

Consider, for example, the problem of *anorexia nervosa.* Words like that are not usually used in this book, but anorexia nervosa is becoming so common, especially among teenage girls, that you perhaps have heard the term. It refers to a condition that causes a person to stop eating. At first there may be a simple desire to diet and lose weight, but later the person stops eating almost completely. Sometimes laxatives, forced vomiting, and even hiding food instead of eating it are all used to reduce weight. If this doesn't stop the person could eventually die of starvation. It has happened! Often such people have a lot of insecurity and anxiety about themselves or about the future. If you or a friend begin to show signs of anorexia nervosa, it is wise to get some medical help as soon as you can.

Apart from anorexia nervosa, it is probable that you have seen many of the common reactions to inferiority in some of your friends. Most of us would admit that we even have seen some of these tendencies in ourselves, and we know they don't work very well. So let us consider a better solution.

Challenge Your Own Thinking

Dr. Albert Ellis is a New York psychologist who has written a number of books and become well-known as a counselor and speaker. Some of his ideas are strongly anti-Christian and a lot of people disagree with many of his conclusions, but some of what he says makes a lot of sense.

Ellis maintains, for example, that we all talk to ourselves all the time. We don't do it out loud, of course, but we do tell ourselves things like *I'm no good, I'm stupid, I'm a failure,* or *I'll never succeed in anything.*

Sometimes these ideas are not our own. They come from our relatives, our teachers, or even our past experiences. Nevertheless, we recite them to ourselves so often that after a while we begin to believe them.

Whenever we find ourselves saying these things we need to ask ourselves two questions: *Is what I'm saying really true? If it is true, does it really matter?*

I know a man who, as a teenager, was convinced by his mother that he was a very poor carpenter. When this man got married, he never fixed anything around the house because he believed that he had no carpentry skills. His wife didn't like sawing boards and hammering nails, so she began to challenge her husband's thinking. "Who says you can't do carpentry?" she asked gently. "Have you been convincing yourself of something that isn't true?" My friend began to try some carpentry and found that he could do pretty well. He's not the best, but he's not nearly as bad as he had thought.

Maybe this says something about you. When you hear yourself saying, *I can't,* or, *I'm no good,* ask yourself, *Says who?* You might discover that you have been talking yourself into something that isn't true.

Then ask yourself something else. *Suppose I am incompetent in some areas? Is this really bad? Will the world end because I'm not the best?*

When you start challenging yourself like this, you become less uptight, and life becomes much more relaxed. Then you can follow our final suggestion.

Develop Your Strengths and the Abilities You've Got

What are your strong points and abilities? Write them down and then ask some people who know you well what they think. Remember that nobody is good at everything, but we all have at least some strong points, and we can start building on these.

If you're muscially inclined, try to become a better musician. If you're a capable student, work to get good grades.

If you're an athlete, practice your skills to be better.

Many years ago, before the start of rock music, somebody composed a popular song with an old tune but a pretty modern message: "You've got to do with what you got, and never mind how much you've got."

You may not be good-looking, but at least you can be neat.

You may not be too smart, but you can do your best.

You may be a poor athlete, but you can try to do well, encourage those who have good ability, and then put more of your energy on doing the things you do better than sports.

In working to develop your strengths, be careful of pride. If you get too capable in one area you might find yourself putting down others and becoming like those Pharisees who thought they were too good for others.

Also, be careful not to forget people. You can get so caught up in your music, after-school job, sports, study, or other activities that you withdraw into your own little world. Then you might not feel inferior, but you don't have any friends and that's another stress.

A lot of people never get over their feelings of inferiority. If they were novelists writing a description of themselves, the picture would be mostly bad. But you don't have to keep knocking yourself down. You can start now to deal with the stress of not liking yourself. Maybe you should learn to love yourself, as God loves you. Don't forget that He can help you to like and respect yourself more than you do now.

8

Emotional Stress:
Handling Your Feelings

Vance Havner must be an interesting man. I've never met him, but I know he's led a long, full life. He preached his first sermon when he was twelve and has spent most of his life traveling, speaking in churches, and writing books.

I doubt that most teenagers would get very excited about Vance Havner's books. They're not filled with adventure, and his language is that of a man approaching the end of life, not the words of somebody young and vigorous.

You might be interested, however, in Mr. Havner's conclusions about the three kinds of days that most of us encounter as we go through life. Sometimes we have what he calls *mountaintop days,* when things are going really well. It is then that we are happy, enthusiastic, and feeling good about everything.

Nobody goes through life like that all the time, however. Mixed in with the mountaintop days are a lot of *ordinary days,* when we push on with the usual grind. At such times we're not especially happy but neither are we sad. We're not enthusiastic, but we're not bored or down either.

Sometimes we do get down, however, really down, and these are what might be called the *dark days.* Most of us know about these times. We feel sad, angry (at others or at ourselves), lazy, bored, and sometimes dragging along with a "what's-the-use?" attitude. When dark days come we often decide that nobody likes us, that we are no good, and that there isn't much real purpose for living.

Notice that in describing these three kinds of days we've been talking mostly about *feelings*—of happiness, excitement, sadness, disappointment, anger, and boredom. I could also have mentioned fear, worry, loneliness, or jealousy. These are all emotions that everybody feels, which can affect us a great deal, and which sometimes create a lot of stress.

It's Okay to Have Feelings

For some reason many people in our culture have the idea that feelings are bad—especially if we show them. As little kids we are expected to stifle our emotions (especially when we go to the dentist), and we soon learn that "big boys don't cry," even if they want to.

Surely there is something unnatural about this idea that feelings should be squelched. When God created human beings— and all of our feelings—He called this creation good. He never told us to deny our emotions, and apparently, He expressed feelings Himself. The Bible tells us that God laughs, gets angry, rejoices, and shows compassion. Jesus was often very gentle, but He also got angry, discouraged, and so sad that He cried openly.

Let's start, then, by agreeing that emotions are good. They add variety and interest to life, and they prevent us from living a routine, boring, blah existence. At times, of course, uncontrolled emotions can pull us down into depression or push us into angry outbursts that we regret later. But this doesn't mean that feelings in themselves are bad. Quite the opposite is true.

Feelings May Be More Intense During the Teen Years

I can't prove this, but it seems that everything is felt with greater intensity when you are a teenager. When you get older, you're more used to disappointment, sadness, loneliness, and grief. You see the world a little differently and are able to recognize that life goes on in spite of its frustrations. When you're younger, however, things hit you with greater force because they're new. You may never have failed before, or been in love, or grieved, so these things really pack a punch when they come.

Have you ever been separated from a close friend because one of the families moved? It's easy for older people to say, "You'll get over it"—and you probably will—but nothing seems able to reduce the pain when you first are separated by that moving van. There is hurt, anger, loneliness, sadness, and deep longing—all at the same time.

Because your feelings are so strong, your reactions to the feelings might be strong as well. Little things, which might not bother you later, really irritate you now and can lead to explosions of anger—especially directed toward your brothers or sisters. Disappointments and failures can plunge you into such great depression that you even consider suicide—all over issues that might not seem so bad when you look back on them later. On the brighter side of life, kids have been known to do some crazy things to celebrate their joy over something like a football victory which really isn't all that important. Adults, I should add, also can get carried away when the hometown team wins. Notice, for example, how some otherwise calm men and women can get pretty excited about the World Series, Super Bowl, or Stanley Cup.

I think it would help if parents could understand the strength of teenager's feelings. It can also help you to understand yourself and others better when emotions begin to make themselves felt in your life.

It Can Be Unhealthy to Squelch Feelings

I have a friend who really is annoyed by his younger brother. In addition to being a pest, the younger brother seems to get privileges that my friend never had, and to make matters worse, the parents seem to be playing favorites. When we discussed this recently my friend made an interesting statement:

"I don't like what's going on at home. I don't think it's fair, but I've decided I won't get mad."

I admire my friend's determination to keep cool, but in fact he already *is* mad whether he recognizes this or not. If we could measure what is happening within his body we'd see that whenever he thinks about his brother, my friend's muscles are tense, his blood pressure has gone up, his heart may be beating faster, and there are chemical changes in his bloodstream.

When animals feel threatened they either run and hide or they fight. In either case their bodies become alert and ready to spring into action. The same is true with human bodies. They automatically respond to feelings and get us ready to act.

This puts human beings into a dilemma that most animals never face. If we give vent to our feelings and let them take over, we can get into all kinds of trouble. We might say or do things that could get others mad, cause a fight, and make us feel guilty or sorry later. All of this could even bring us into conflict with the law.

But isn't the alternative bad as well? If we squelch our feelings, anger and frustration can fester inside, the body might stay tense (this can lead to a variety of physical illnesses), and we can develop the inner bitterness which, according to the Bible, "causes deep trouble," including personal problems (Hebrews 12:15).

With almost every emotion, then, we are faced with a deci-sion—*Do I let it out or hold it in?* Sometimes the decision is easy. If you're at a football game and the team is winning you have no hesitation in cheering enthusiastically.

But what if the team loses and you feel like crying?

What if you are really angry? Do you let it out or hold it in?

What if you are disappointed, lonely, or guilty? How do you handle feelings then?

Feelings Can Be Handled

Have you ever been in a classroom or (even worse) in church when you got "the giggles"? Perhaps some little thing happened that got you laughing, and the more you tried to keep a straight face, the harder it became.

I can remember times in church when I'd pull out a handker-chief and pretend to blow my nose, even though I really wanted an opportunity to hide my face and muffle my smirking. Some-times my whole body would shake, and when I felt about to ex-plode I'd cough to cover the laugh. If other kids were present it was worse. Our whole bodies would tremble as we tried to keep from laughing out loud, and when someone else would cough or smirk, we'd all get started again—often when there wasn't even anything funny to laugh at.

During those times I'd try to think of things that were not funny—like the history test on Monday, the lawn that needed to be cut, or even the sermon. Getting my mind on something else often helped, especially if my friends were able to control them-selves as well.

A little thing, like trying to stifle a giggle, can show that feelings are difficult to control. They *can* be controlled, how-ever, in ways that do not require you to squelch them but which also prevent them from taking over and overwhelming you.

First, you handle feelings by admitting that they are there. If you're disappointed, mad, or glad, admit it—at least to yourself and to God.

Second, think before you act. There's value in the old idea of counting to ten before you explode. Often this is all the time you need to stop yourself from doing or saying something you might regret later.

But it isn't easy to stop your feelings and actions. Have you ever had someone tell you to stop being jealous or disappointed? Have you ever heard the words "You really shouldn't feel angry," stated in a syrupy voice by someone who clearly didn't know how mad you felt inside? Have you ever tried to tell yourself to stop feeling depressed or guilty? If the answer to any of these questions is yes, then you probably have discovered that feelings don't go away just because you or someone else decides that they should.

The only way we can change feelings is to deal with the issues and ideas that cause our emotions in the first place.

Let's go back to my friend who is annoyed by his younger brother. Yelling at his brother or parents will only make matters worse, so my friend needs to use his brain to answer some questions.

What specific things bother me about my brother?

Which things can I ignore since they aren't important enough to fight over?

How can I change in ways that will help solve the problem?

How can my brother change, and what can I do to bring this about?

How could I get my parents to help?

This means using your God-given brain to think through a problem before you make matters worse by overreacting. Often a friend, parent, or counselor can help you decide on some course of action if you are not able to think this through yourself.

At some time you will also need to recognize a third approach to handling feelings: express them carefully. When you do this, try to respect the opinions and emotions of others.

Before I even started to write this book I presented all of the ideas to a group of teenagers, most of whom listened politely but didn't say much about whether or not it was helpful. One night, however, we had a question-and-answer session, and the first comment came from a brilliant girl named Linda.

"This is all very interesting, but . . ."

I could see she was choosing her words carefully.

"This is all very interesting, but does it really work—in *your* life, for example?"

That was a good question, and I tried to answer honestly.

Like everyone else, including you, I feel emotion. I enjoy being with my family, but sometimes I get mad, forget my own advice, and yell.

When that happens, I quickly apologize and try to express my feelings in a more helpful way. I tell them when I feel angry, disappointed, sad, or especially happy. I try to find out why these feelings have come, and sometimes my teenagers and I try together to get to the root of the problem and solve it.

Notice that we don't deny feelings, pretending that they don't exist. We try to express them honestly and then consider what we can do to handle them.

What to Do About Anger

Anger is one of the hardest emotions to control, especially when you are a teenager and can't always control the things or people that make you mad.

It might surprise you to know that the Bible says a lot about anger. Consider, for example, the following words (from Ephesians 4:26, 27, 31, 32):

If you are angry, don't sin by nursing your grudge. Don't let the sun go down with you still angry—get over it quickly; for when you are angry you give a mighty foothold to the devil. . . . Quarreling, harsh words, and dislike of others should have no place in your lives. Instead, be kind to each other, tenderhearted, forgiving one another, just as God has forgiven you because you belong to Christ.

This is good advice:

- Admit your anger when it comes.
- Think about your anger and try to do something about it, right away, instead of letting it turn into a grudge.
- Stop yourself from quarreling and unkindness (you can let others know you're mad without hurting them).
- Try treating others with kindness (this dissolves anger quickly—it's hard for others to be mad at you if you are doing something nice, and it is difficult to be mad at others if you are treating them with sincere kindness).
- Forgive others when they wrong you (holding a grudge can hurt you more than them).
- Remember that if you are a Christian, you belong to Christ who has promised to help you deal with your anger. Talk to Him about this.

These are not easy guidelines to follow, especially when you are really mad. You might have to read over this section again in the future, and at times you may want to talk to a friend or counselor about your anger. Even if you learn to handle feelings, if you're like most people there probably will be times in the future when you "lose your cool." At such times, God forgives and enables us to learn from our failures. We can even learn how to handle our anger better in the future.

What to Do When You're Depressed and Blue

Do you remember how we started this book—describing a place known as the suicide belt? As you probably know, suicide is a major cause of death among teenagers, and most teenagers who attempt suicide are reacting to feelings of depression.

Recently I was sitting in a restaurant discussing plans for this book with a man who works a lot with high school students. I don't think our conversation was loud, but it soon became clear that the lady at a nearby table was eavesdropping. I lowered my voice, but she seemed to listen even more intently. Then she did something I wasn't expecting.

After draining her coffee cup, slipping into her coat, and picking up her bill, she came over to our table.

"Excuse me," she began somewhat hesitatingly. "I really didn't mean to listen in on your conversation, but the issue of teenage suicide is pretty close to me. My daughter killed herself last summer, apparently because she was depressed. I didn't expect it, and it has been awfully hard to keep going since it happened."

We talked for a few minutes more, and then my friend and I watched as the lady left the restaurant—alone.

I wonder what caused the daughter's depression—or what makes anyone get depressed. There can be several causes.

Sometimes depression has a physical cause. The problem may be in our glands or blood. There may be a tumor or a virus dragging us down emotionally. More often, the physical cause may be lack of exercise, a poor diet, or insufficient sleep. Almost everyone has had the experience of being irritable and discouraged after missing sleep during a long weekend or while studying for an exam.

Depression can also come when we have had a loss. As we saw in an earlier chapter, the breakup of our parents' marriage or grief over the death of someone important can play havoc with our emotions. We also feel sadness when we lose a job, a chance to win something, a friend who moves away, or even a pet. Many teenagers, and older people as well, have felt the depression that comes with sickness, which, of course, means a loss of health.

Perhaps you know the story of Joni Eareckson, a healthy teenager who made a two-second mistake by diving into a shallow part of Chesapeake Bay. Her head hit bottom, she broke her neck, and she has been paralyzed from the neck down ever since. This severe loss of good health, to put it mildly, was very depressing.

This leads us to another cause of depression—feelings of helplessness. Most of us can keep going in a difficult situation—if we think things will change. But what if there seems to be no hope? What if teachers never understand, algebra never makes any sense, your physical appearance never changes, or your parents never seem to let up on their criticisms? At such times you can feel very helpless, and this can pull you down.

Before long you may begin to feel sad, tired, bored, and sometimes guilty. You might be smiling all the time so nobody suspects you are down, but inside you are hurting, unable to concentrate, and probably very angry. Some depressed people are irritable, daydream, have frequent headaches, a tendency to pull away from others, and an unusual resistance to attending school or work. All of this can signal depression.

You may have discovered that it is easy to get depressed but it isn't easy to recover.

You can start by talking to yourself—trying to find the causes of your down feelings. Perhaps you can do something about your health or feelings of emptiness over some loss. Maybe your situation is not as helpless as you think. If you're like me, when you feel depressed you'll ask, *Am I angry about something?* You may discover that anger bottled up inside is pulling you down. Ask yourself what can be done to change your situation and your outlook.

Let me give you a warning, however. When you are really down it is pretty hard to think like this. Often you don't have the energy or the desire. At such times, suicide may seem like the easiest way out.

Even if you've never thought of suicide, it can help to talk with a sensitive person who can encourage, understand, and help you out of your bind. Your parents or a close friend may be able to help, but you probably will find that some other adult is better. Think of the most understanding person you know. Then go talk with that person. In all of this, don't forget to pray. God, who created emotions, surely understands and helps when we feel overwhelmed with depression.

Some Concluding Thoughts About Fear

Everybody knows that little children show a lot of fears, but as we get older we tend to hide our fears and pretend that they don't exist.

But they do exist! Some of our childhood fears may be gone, but new ones have come instead. At times we are all afraid of failure or change. Most people are afraid of being embarrassed, and some fear getting too close to members of the opposite sex. (Not all teens have that problem!) Perhaps you also have known people who are afraid of dating, of leaving home, of undressing in a locker room, or of trying anything new.

Fears, then, are very common—even among teenagers who like to keep them hidden. It is best to admit them honestly (at least to ourselves), recognizing that most of the things we fear don't happen. It also helps to discuss our fears with someone who can give us a different perspective. And remember to pray. God, who is love, enables us to handle our fears (and other emotions) so that we can live life without crippling emotional stress.

Before we leave the topic of feelings, let me remind you of something you may have overlooked. Even if emotional stresses do not bother you much, there may be other teens in your school, church, neighborhood, or home who are under a lot of stress because of their feelings. These people need kindness, not criticism;

acceptance, not condemnation. Be careful that your jokes don't cut or tear down others, and try to remember that your mountaintop days may be dark days for someone else. The more we can help and respect one another, the better it will be for everyone as we struggle with the stresses that come from our feelings.

9

Sexual Stress:
Handling Your Hormones

Many centuries ago, there lived a curious king who wondered what language children would speak if they never heard anyone talk. Would they speak Hebrew, Latin, Greek, or even some unheard-of language (like English)? Would they use the language of their parents?

To find out, the king ordered all mothers to raise their babies in complete silence. There was to be no laughter, baby talk, or even adult conversation when the infants were present.

As you might have guessed, the experiment didn't work very well because all the babies died. The old king had discovered something that we modern people all know to be true: In order to grow up normally, little children need attention, love, acceptance, and physical contact with others.

For some reason, however, in our society we seem to think that closeness—especially physical closeness—isn't needed after your second or third birthday. Adults may pat kids on the head as a sign of affection, but as we get older, most of us don't touch much. We keep at a safe distance from other people, and guys especially don't hug each other unless somebody scores a touchdown in a football game. If your school has a bad team, you might have to wait a long time for a hug!

On one of my trips overseas, I was met at the airport by a man who shook my hand and then just held on. For the next five minutes we walked around the airport holding hands, much to my awkward embarrassment. It sure was a relief to spot my luggage so I could hold hands with my old familiar suitcase. Only later did I learn that it is not unusual for people of the same sex to hold hands in the Orient. Such hand holding has no more sexual meaning than a kiss on the cheek from your fifty-eight-year-old, bald, bachelor uncle. But my oriental friends may have discovered something that the rest of us should learn: All human beings need closeness, acceptance, and at least periodic physical contact with other human beings.

That issue of physical contact can create a lot of tension during the teenage years. Teens are at a time in life when their bodies have a surge of sexual development along with all the physical and emotional changes that come as you move into adulthood. Partly because of these physical changes, kids who never thought at all about sex a few years before, suddenly find themselves thinking about it a great deal.

When all of these inner physical changes take place, we begin to discover that our world seems to have a crazy preoccupation with sex. Movies, popular music, novels, television programs, and advertisements often make repeated references to sex. Unless you are a hermit, this adult-dominated society hits you with sexual messages everywhere you turn. That, coupled with your emerging sexual drives and your natural need for closeness, can make sexual stress a big problem.

In this chapter I want to mention some things that might be helpful as you grapple with your growing sexual urges. I don't plan to criticize, condemn, embarrass, or create guilt in you. I probably won't be able to answer all of your questions either, but at least let me suggest several conclusions about sex which you might want to consider.

1. God Created Sex and Said It Was Good

According to the Bible, when God created males and females He looked over His work and announced that it was good. Instead of making us unisex creatures, He gave us male and female bodies which can fit together beautifully. He gave us hormones and sexual urges, even though He knew that these same hormones might cause problems later for people who live in sexually perverted societies like ours. When Adam and Eve first met in the garden they were stark naked and God told them to "be fruitful and multiply." He knew that sex would sometimes bring babies, but He also wanted it to bring pleasure and enjoyment.

Most of the good things in this life can be misused, however, so the Bible has given us warnings about sexual "looseness." Since the warnings are both precise and strong, it is clear that according to our Creator, sex apart from marriage really is very destructive, whether we agree or not. (For example, look at the following Bible verses: 1 Corinthians 6:18; Ephesians 5:3–7; 1 Thessalonians 4:2–8; Hebrews 13:4. Try to read these in a modern translation.) The same God who created sex and called it good gives no grounds for promiscuity or the sex games which can occupy time and attention at parties or in the backseats of cars.

2. God Has Given Us Standards for Living a Great Life

One day when He was talking to some of His followers, Jesus mentioned that He had come to earth to give us "life in all its fullness." He didn't want to make our lives miserable, or boring, or dull. He wanted us to have the best. He still does.

That is why He has told us to respect one another. The Bible tells us to encourage, build up, and be kind to others. We are told to avoid sin, to be like Christ, and to keep sexual intercourse within marriage. All of this is not to make us frustrated and angry. It is for our own good.

You may have heard this example a million times, but perhaps it's worth reminding you how parents watch over their toddlers. The child may scream for freedom to go where he or she wants, even if this means wandering into the busy street. But the parents say, "No, not now." This is because those parents know about the dangers of traffic, and they want what is best for the child. God is a loving parent. That's why He gives us standards and restraints—even though we might choose to buck and ignore them.

3. We Live in a Society That Ignores God's Standards

After completing a big survey of teenage sexuality, a writer recently predicted that within a few years only three kinds of people would remain virgins through the teen years and on to the time of marriage: the deeply religious, the emotionally disturbed, and the personally undesirable. Put in less flowery language, this seems to say that unless you're a fanatic, crazy, or ugly, you'll have sexual intercourse at least once before you reach twenty.

Please don't believe that conclusion!

Before I started writing this chapter, I read a lot about teenage sex and one thing became very clear: Although many teens do have sex either occasionally or repeatedly (everyone knows that), a lot of normal teens *do not* have sex before marriage. It isn't at all uncommon or weird to decide that you'll remain a virgin until marriage, and it isn't unusual for people to stick with this decision.

According to a University of California psychologist who has written a book on teenage sex, teenagers do fall in love and like all people they have desires for closeness and intimacy. Nevertheless, "there isn't nearly as much casual sex going on as adults believe there to be." Most young people think about a lot of other things besides sex according to this psychologist, and in spite of what some parents fear, the whole teenage population is not looking for opportunities to jump into bed with anybody who is willing and available.

Those teens who do get involved sexually probably do so for a number of reasons.

Many don't know about the Bible's teaching on sex. Others don't care, and some choose to ignore their religious teachings, at least for a while. It isn't surprising that even without thinking much about it, many young people get swallowed up by the sexual looseness of the society in which we live. We are surrounded by X-rated movies and books, explicit and less obvious references to sex on television, pressure from peers, and the fact that almost everyone has access to a car—that mobile bedroom which gives us privacy and whisks us away from the gaze of disapproving parents.

Some teens probably use sex as a weapon to get even with parents, the church, or perhaps with somebody who has jilted them in the past. (If you think about this for a while, you'll probably conclude that when sex is used to get revenge, everybody loses.)

Other teens, those who are starved for love and acceptance think that sex—even for a few minutes—will give them the closeness they want so much. This may be the saddest kind of sex, because self-centered individuals often take advantage of the teenager who craves intimacy. After the sexual act is over, the couple separates, and the love-starved victim is left feeling emptier than ever.

If you believe in the devil, as I do, you will recognize that there is another reason for sexual looseness among teens. The Bible calls Satan the father of lies and he must be behind most of the excuses that people use to give the green light to sex:

"Everybody's doing it!"

"If it feels good, it must be okay."

"Once you start you can't stop—so why try stopping!"

"Sex apart from marriage is no big deal. It's just a physical response."

"At some time we all need to let off our sexual tension."

Like all lies, these statements have a little truth mixed in with the error. The same could be said about the biggest lie of all—that sex never does any harm.

4. Sex Apart From God's Plans Creates Problems

To be honest, it is hard to prove that easy sex creates problems. This is because the problems don't always show up immediately.

When I was a teenager, they told us that there were three reasons for avoiding sex: pregnancy, venereal disease, and guilt. Some people now say that these three reasons no longer exist, but such a conclusion is not backed up by the facts.

I won't bore you with statistics except to say that teenage pregnancies and venereal disease have almost become epidemics within the past few years, and guilt seems to be a problem with many kids.

Consider pregnancies, for example. One million teenage girls get pregnant every year. Why don't they use contraceptives? Some teenagers are too young or embarrassed to get hold of birth-control devices. Other teenagers just don't like to use them. Then, even when they are used, some people discover that they don't always work (no birth-control method works 100 percent of the time). Other teens may be like Sherry, who was pictured in the newspaper holding her baby.

"I really didn't think about birth control," she said. "I knew about it, but this was the first time my boyfriend and I had gone out together. We hadn't planned to have sex." Perhaps you've heard stories like that yourself.

Even if birth control was always reliable and venereal disease was abolished forever, what about the emotional costs of premarital sex? What about the remorse and self-condemnation? Here again there are differences between people and there are not many statistics. But counselors and magazine articles both keep coming up with the same conclusions—a lot of people feel tremendous guilt, regret, and sadness after sex, especially when they have used or been used by another human being.

Often these feelings bring about tension between the couple. "Why do I feel so lousy about this?" one teenager wrote. "It wasn't Jane's fault. It was mine. I told her that if a girl really cares for a fellow she should prove it. But I kept telling myself if she was the right kind of girl she would have stopped me." She didn't, and now sex has driven a wedge between them, increased tension, and caused them to lose respect for each other.

Ann Landers gets thousands of letters from teenagers and many of these are concerned with sex. One of the saddest came from a girl who wrote the following:

Dear Ann Landers:

I am 17 and already my life is messed up. Ted and I went steady for six months and we began to do things we had no right to do. I became pregnant.

We both quit school and got married right away. My folks thought it would be best if we moved out of town, so we did. I despise my life and what I have done to Ted. The baby cries all the time and gets on Ted's nerves. He drinks too much and I can't blame him. We live in a dump and there is no money for sitters or movies or decent clothes. Ted never says anything but I know he must hate me because I got him into this. I'm afraid he hates the baby, too. He never pays attention to her.

There are times when I think this is all a bad dream and I'll wake up at home, get dressed and go to school with the kids I liked so much. But I know too well that those days are over for me and I am stuck.

I'm not writing for advice. It's too late for that. I'm just writing in the hope that you will print this letter for the benefit of other teenagers who think they know it all—like I did.

—Wrecked at 17.

This is an extreme case, but might there be many more like it? The writer of the letter has learned what the Bible taught many years ago: Sex in itself is not bad or dirty, but it can become as powerful and destructive as dynamite. When used for our own selfish pleasure, it eventually explodes and hurts. It is impossible to mature psychologically if we treat sex as a harmless toy we share with playmates and can play with whenever we feel in the mood. If you are a Christian you can't ignore God's standards for sexual purity and expect to grow spiritually.

5. Sex Is Something More Than Intercourse

Several years ago, many schools began teaching courses in sex education. In most cases, the people who started this had good intentions. They wanted to give accurate facts about sex because they knew that many teenagers don't know as much about sex as they think they do.

Not all of these teachers recognized that *sex is not the same as love.* (I wonder why we talk about "making love" when really we mean having sexual intercourse?) Love is something deep, involving respect, admiration, and a desire to give. Often love doesn't involve sex at all.

Sex is a biological response, but it involves more than something physical. Sex is tied in with our ways of thinking, our views of religion, our feelings, and even our career choices. For some people, sex is a way to escape loneliness and find acceptance. Other people use sex to manipulate one another or to avoid talking to people who are not interesting. Most young people find that sex forces us to think about what is right and wrong. Sex also creates a lot of pressure, but this pressure can be handled.

6. Sex Can Be Controlled

When she was interviewed by *Newsweek* magazine, a sixteen-year-old girl concluded that "it must have been a lot easier when society set sex standards for you." It probably was also a lot more frustrating to have a list of do's and don'ts—and I bet kids in those days tried to buck the rules and get around them, just as all of us have done at times, and as teenagers have been doing since the start of history.

Nobody likes rules, but if there is one thing to keep in mind about sex it is this: *Don't let yourself get into situations where you might lose self-control.* That is a hard guideline to follow because sometimes we're surprised at where and when we get "turned on," and often we don't want to stop. Nevertheless, the real mark of a maturing person is that he or she is learning self-control. To do this you might keep the following ideas in mind.

Stay away from books, magazines, and movies that are sexually arousing. These only put ideas into your mind and get you stirred up.

Try to avoid sexual fantasy. We can't stop what pops into our minds, but we don't have to keep mulling over dirty thoughts. When we get into the habit of undressing people mentally, for example, it becomes easier to do the same thing in reality if we get the chance.

Steer clear of tempting situations. Parked cars, lonely beaches, or houses where nobody else is home are dangerous. When two people are alone, it is easier for emotions to take over—even if you were planning "just to talk." If you just want to talk, go to some place where talking won't give way to other more intimate activities.

Avoid sexually arousing people. Keep a wide circle of friends and try to avoid too much contact with any one person who "turns you on." If you feel yourself becoming exceptionally fond of somebody, and chemistry seems to be winning over judgment, break the habit by dating someone else to change the routine. *Recognize the dangers in heavy petting.* This is hard to stop once you get started, since it is natural to keep wanting more. I agree with the person who wrote that we should keep all hands outside of clothing and all four feet on the floor. If the kisses are making you too weak to sit up, then it's time to quit. *You* can take the responsibility for stopping (don't leave this to the other person). Keep vertical at all times.

Try to think of some nonsexual ways to enjoy each other and to express love. Shopping together, spending time with other couples, helping one another with homework or projects around the house, even praying for each other can all be meaningful and fun. If you need sex in order to get along now, you have a pretty lopsided and unhealthy relationship. Someday, if you get married, you'll discover that sex is only a part of a healthy husband-wife relationship.

Ann Landers has mentioned two additional suggestions for "cooling it."

A girl should not go out with a boy unless she has introduced him to her parents. A girl who would allow herself to be picked up in a drug store or a movie, in a park, or off the street is taking a frightening chance—not to mention the fact that her reputation will be mud when the word gets around.

Also, if your parents have not set a curfew for you, set one for yourself. It never is sound to go out for the evening figuring that you'll go home when the fun is over.

Finally, and most important, *ask God to help you.* Saint Paul was unmarried when he wrote his New Testament epistles and maybe he was as tempted sexually as you are. He knew that "sexual immorality, impurity . . . orgies, and the like" are all part of our sinful nature. But when we allow God's Holy Spirit to control our lives we begin to develop the self-control that we don't have otherwise (Galatians 5:19–23 NIV). God will help, especially if you do your part in steering clear of avoidable temptations.

7. You Can Be Free of Guilt

When I was learning to become a psychologist, I once worked for several months in a mental hospital. One day, in the cafeteria, I had a long talk with a counselor who had been working in the hospital for years. He told me something very interesting.

"The biggest problem for most of the people in this place is that they can't accept forgiveness."

After a while, guilt becomes like a cancer. It eats out our insides, destroying all our enthusiasm and zest for living.

But it doesn't have to be like that.

If you feel guilty about sex (or about anything else) then try the following.

Ask God to forgive you. There is no limit to how much or how often He will forgive. According to the Bible (1 John 1:9), "If we confess our sins to him, he can be depended on to forgive us and to cleanse us from every wrong. [And it is perfectly proper for God to do this for us because Christ died to wash away our sins.]" Don't be afraid to tell God about your problems and ask Him to forgive. He knows everything before you tell Him, and He has already promised to give His forgiveness no matter what you have done.

Make up your mind to avoid wrongdoing in the future.

Try to repair wrongdoing from the past. This might mean asking forgiveness from some other person, fixing something you have broken, or paying back money that you owe.

Forgive the other person. It is easy to carry a burden of resentment. If you keep such an attitude of revenge and bitterness, you'll discover sooner or later that *you* are the one who suffers and feels most miserable.

If the guilt feelings stay, talk to somebody about them. Try to find an older, more mature Christian who is understanding and who knows about God's forgiveness. Even a friend can give you help and encouragement, but be careful who you choose and don't make the mistake of telling your problems to everybody. When you do find somebody, it may be hard sharing your struggles, but this can also be tremendously helpful. When you share, you get rid of the bottled-up pressures, and it really helps to find acceptance from somebody else who cares.

Decide to be a caring person yourself. One of the best ways to help ourselves is to help others. Don't force yourself on people, making yourself obnoxious. Instead, look around. Is there some way you can serve others? You might start at home where (if your house is like mine) something always needs to be done.

A Postscript on Masturbation

One of the greatest of all teenage sexual stresses is the problem of masturbation—stimulating your own genitals to bring sexual pleasure. I suppose I've read dozens of articles on this subject and they reach all kinds of conclusions. At one extreme is the view that masturbation is always a sin that must be stopped somehow. Other people say that masturbation is no big problem and might even be a gift from God to keep us from sexual intercourse. How, then, do we deal with such differences in opinion?

To begin, let's accept the facts that masturbation is common (especially among males) and does not harm us physically, but that it does arouse guilt in a lot of people.

The Bible, which says something about almost every other sexual struggle, says nothing about masturbation. This doesn't mean that masturbation is right or that it is something we've only discovered in the twentieth century. In previous centuries, people got married earlier, but I suspect kids struggled with masturbation then, just as they do now.

Is masturbation wrong? I wish somebody could give a clear, concise answer to that question, but I wonder if that is possible. Some of the fantasies that go with masturbation are wrong.

We're just making the problem worse when we think about self-ish pleasures, perversions, intercourse with people we know, or sex with strangers we notice at school or on the street. The Bible comes down pretty hard on such lust.

For some people, masturbation is wrong because it becomes a way of withdrawing from people and avoiding problems. But that's not a problem for everyone who masturbates.

Then there are the people who feel that masturbation helps them release tension, although for some it just creates stress—the more they masturbate, the more they want to do it again.

Also, for a lot of people, masturbation brings guilt which can make them discouraged and disgusted with themselves. One survey concluded that while half of all teens feel little or no guilt, the other 50 percent are bothered by guilt feelings about masturbation.

How we feel about masturbation, however, still says nothing about whether it is wrong. Eichmann, the man who killed thousands of Jews in a Nazi prison camp, claimed that he never felt guilty about his actions, even though he clearly was a murderer. On the other hand, I know people who feel guilty about things they've never done. Your feelings about masturbation, therefore, might not be the best indication of whether or not it is okay.

There is one conclusion that probably everybody accepts: Masturbation is a second-best kind of sex. It is selfish and not at all close to God's ideal for marriage. Let's agree also that masturbation is hard to stop.

So what can you do about it?

Over the centuries there have been all kinds of answers to that question: Take cold showers! Wear yourself out by jogging or playing football. Get so busy that you have no time to think about sex. But none of these work very well, although there *can* be some value in getting involved with people and activities instead of sitting at home alone, thinking about masturbating.

A more common approach is to use willpower. Make up your mind to quit. As you may have discovered, this almost never works. It gets you thinking more about the problem, it makes you anxious, and then—after thinking of an excuse for doing it *just one more time*—you get mad at yourself because you failed again.

It is better to go back to pages 113–114 and read again what we said about self-control. Most of that applies to masturbation.

Then, you can ask yourself if masturbation is hiding some other problem—such as loneliness or shyness. If so, ask your school counselor or youth leader to help with the problem.

You also can keep a clear view in mind about the beauty of sex as God intended. Loathing yourself and hating sex because you masturbate is a sad distraction from the ideal which God created.

Then, ask God to help not only with your masturbation but with your tendency to think sexually impure thoughts. Don't forget that He understands even masturbation, and He forgives.

Finally, recognize that some people never seem able to quit. I'll be criticized for saying that, but I think it is realistic. Even if it stays around in your life, masturbation can become much less frequent and much less of a problem as you grow older.

What About Homosexuality?

Probably we would all be surprised if we knew how many people—including some people you know—struggle every day with homosexual desires. Unlike masturbation, homosexuality is mentioned in the Bible, and the message is clear: Homosexual acts are wrong! It isn't right to be involved sexually with some-one of the same sex.

Probably non-Christians won't accept that conclusion, and there even are some Christians who feel that if you tend to be gay you should be open about it and give in to your tendencies. But that view can't be defended from the Bible.

Some books say that if you have homosexual desires, it's your own fault. I disagree. Nobody sits down at about age twelve or thirteen and decides whether to be "turned on" by the opposite sex or the same sex. At some time in life we each wake up to the fact that, probably as a result of past experiences, we either like girls best, or boys.

Whether you are attracted to males, to females, or even to both, remember that we all have a responsibility to develop self-control. Homosexuals and heterosexuals both get tempted, and both must learn to resist.

If you have homosexual tendencies, ask God to help you keep pure and away from self-pity. Ask Him to change your desires and ask Him, too, to lead you to some more mature Christian with whom you can talk about these tendencies.

Talking to someone can be risky. Your pastor, for example, might be supportive and helpful, but he could also be shocked and inclined to condemn. If you can find a person who is sensitive and caring, however, you can talk through the problem and think about how this affects your life and your relationships with others.

Some Final Words on Sex

Sometimes I think we take something beautiful that God created and make it the biggest problem in our lives. Of course sex can be a problem and a big stress, but for many teens it isn't an overwhelming issue. It is one of many pressures but it isn't the only stress, and in a lot of cases it is not the biggest stress.

Have you ever wondered how Jesus must have handled sex? He was the most normal, well-balanced, and fulfilled person who ever walked on this earth, but He wasn't married and He never had sexual intercourse. He had all the temptations and pressures that you and I have, but He never gave in.

The reason for this can be found in the Bible. The next time you are tempted, think about these words from 1 Corinthians 10:13.

> ... the wrong desires that come into your life aren't anything new and different. Many others have faced exactly the same problems before you. And no temptation is irresistible. You can trust God to keep the temptation from becoming so strong that you can't stand up against it, for he has promised this and will do what he says. He will show you how to escape temptation's power so that you can bear up patiently against it.

10

Religious Stress: Thinking Through the Things You Believe

Not long ago I received a book in the mail written by Paul Vitz, a psychology professor in New York. The book, *Psychology As Religion: The Cult of Self-Worship,* talked about religion in the world today, and the author had some interesting things to say about what people believe.

A lot of us go to church, he suggested, but really aren't much interested in worshiping God, learning how to pray, or finding out what the Bible says.

Instead many who attend church today are interested mostly in visiting their friends and learning about themselves. Some teenagers—perhaps you—don't consider themselves to be very religious and if they go to church at all it's to please some friends (often of the opposite sex) or to keep peace at home. The psychologist who wrote about religion even suggested that we have a new religion today. It's not a worship of God. Instead we tend to worship ourselves.

Before you throw out that idea (at first it *does* seem sort of crazy), look at the conclusion reached by Dawson McAllister in an article he wrote for *Worldwide Challenge* magazine:

> "Me" is the most fashionable word in American culture today. Looking out for "number one" ... is a matter of course. Men and women (including teens) are unashamedly lovers of self. A "me-ist" says "I am the center of the universe. I don't need God telling me what to do. I can meet my own needs, take care of myself and enjoy all the pleasures that can be found in self. Absolutes are non-existent. I will become my own value system. I will answer only to me."

You might not have jumped into the "me-first" way of thinking, but millions have. It dominates homes where family members look out for themselves and leave, when they can, if they don't like the family or if they find more interesting people elsewhere. The me-ist religion is proclaimed on TV, where violence, drinking, and sex—almost all self-centered—dominate the programs. Me-ism is seen in the high school lunchroom, the classrooms (where teachers encourage you to do your own thing), and the halls, where in a recent year 5,200 American high school teachers and 282,000 students were beaten up—by people concerned about themselves. The self-centered search for pleasure leads to many of the one million pregnancies that occur every year among unmarried American girls between the ages of fifteen and nineteen.

It is easy to conclude that the me-first attitude applies only to other people, but that probably isn't true. Me-first thinking affects everybody in some way and presents us with some difficult questions.

For example, how should you live in a world that seems to put "me" above God or anyone else?

How do you decide what to believe?

How do you know that God is real and that He cares about individuals?

How can we decide what is right and wrong?

How can we seriously commit ourselves to Christ, when His Church is so often characterized by hypocrisy, phoniness, rigidity, and dullness?

Questions like these are important. The way you answer will determine how you spend your life and maybe how you will spend eons of time after you die. Your answer will also have a bearing on the stresses you face even as a teenager.

If you decide to reject religion or to change religions, this could put you into conflict with your parents and friends.

If you stick with the religion of your childhood, this could stifle your independence, prevent you from asking some important questions, and put you at odds with your friends.

What you believe will probably influence your standards of right and wrong, the vocation you choose, the person you marry, and the way in which you entertain yourself.

Obviously, we can't deal with all of these issues in one little chapter, but let's consider just a few questions. If we can make a start at answering these, this should reduce some religious stress and help you to find answers to some questions for yourself.

Question 1: Does it make sense to be a Christian? Notice that I didn't ask if it makes sense to go to church. I'm asking if it makes sense for a teenager in today's me-centered society to become a sincere follower of Jesus Christ.

I once knew a student—I'll call him Norm—who claimed that he didn't have any beliefs. He boasted about his atheism and wasn't hesitant to laugh at those of us who went to church.

What Norm didn't realize was that everybody has beliefs—even atheists—even Norm.

We assume that God exists (that's a belief), or we believe that He does not exist (that's also a belief).

We believe that a caring God created the world and holds it all together, or we believe that human beings are all alone in a universe without any God in control.

We believe that the Bible is all true, or that it is not.

We believe that Jesus rose from the dead, or we believe that He did not.

I could continue with this list, but by now you've probably got the point. All of us, even atheists, have beliefs about some things. We must decide, then, why we should believe one thing and not something else.

When you were very young, you believed what your parents believed. Probably you never even wondered if their beliefs were right or wrong. You just accepted what you heard. In the words of an old spiritual song, we concluded that the religion which was "good enough for father [and mother] is good enough for me."

As you moved into the teenage years, you began to think about religious questions on your own. Shortly after she turned twelve, my daughter Jan asked a good question one day on the way home from church: "How do we know that our religion is right?" Maybe you've asked the same question about your beliefs and in one sense the answer is simple: You look for the evidence.

Let's suppose that you were on the jury in a murder trial. Witness A gets up and says, "I know the prisoner is guilty because I just feel it inside." Witness B gets up and presents you with the murder weapon, the fingerprints on the gun, and the testimony of some witnesses who saw it all happen. Now who would you be more inclined to believe? I hope you would say "the one who presented the evidence."

The evidence in support of Christianity is very powerful.

Consider, for example, the question of whether the Bible is

true. Almost two hundred years ago the French Institute in Paris came up with a list of eighty-two errors in the Bible that they believed would destroy Christianity. Today none of these "errors" remain. They have all been disproven by science. Discoveries by archaeologists, including many nonbelievers, more and more are confirming that the historical facts recorded in the Bible are accurate.

In 1947 a wandering goat keeper accidentally discovered some old jars in a cave in the Middle East. Tucked in the jars were portions of our Bible which some Jewish scholars apparently had hidden near the end of the first century. This discovery got a lot of people excited because it revealed that our modern Bible is an accurate copy of the earliest manuscripts. Some of the scrolls in those old jars might have been written by people who knew Jesus when He was alive, or who knew someone who had known Him.

I once got a letter from a man who wrote that no Greek or Roman historians had ever heard about Jesus. That's not true. Tacitus, Pliny the Younger, and other non-Christians wrote about Jesus in the first century, and their writings confirm the Bible's facts. When you start adding up the evidence, the case for the Bible being true gets stronger and stronger.

The same thing happens if you think about Jesus' Resurrection from the dead. Over five hundred witnesses saw Him after the Resurrection, but some of the religious leaders didn't want people to believe this. So why didn't they stop the rumors by producing the body? The answer, of course, is that no body was there to be found. It couldn't have been stolen since Roman soldiers were guarding the tomb, and at the time the disciples were so disorganized that they never could have come up with a successful plan to get past the military to steal the body.

But, you might argue, isn't much of the Resurrection story based on the Bible? Surely that's a biased book.

Of course it's biased—all books are—but the Bible is honest enough to describe the faults of early religious leaders as well as their strengths. The different Bible books agree on their description of the Resurrection, and the evidence they present is much stronger than that given by recent books which try to disprove the fact that Jesus rose from the dead.

It is easy to start throwing out your Christian beliefs because you're mad at your parents, because you don't like church, because the religious people you know act like hypocrites, or because you feel squelched and would rather be part of the me-generation. Be careful not to make any stupid decisions, however. Ask some questions and look at the evidence before you change religions or decide that you want to be an atheist. Remember that even atheists believe *something*. You have to decide for yourself.

If you want some help on these issues let me suggest two really good books: Paul Little's *Know Why You Believe* (Inter-Varsity Press, 1967) and Clark Pinnock's *Set Forth Your Case* (Moody Press, 1967). *The Unhappy Secrets of the Christian Life* by Philip Yancey and Tim Stafford (Zondervan/Campus Life, 1979) can also help if you are concerned about issues like miracles, hypocrites, and doubt.

As you think about these things and ask God to help you reach some conclusions, I suspect you'll find that it really does make sense to be a Christian.

But another religious question can still create problems for you.

Question 2: What about the hypocrites in the Church?   Hypocrites are people who say they believe one thing but whose lives show something else. Most often they are people who pretend to be religious but really are not.

If you are bothered by these people, you are not alone. Most of us don't like hypocrites, and as you probably know, one of the biggest critics of hypocrisy was Jesus. He didn't have much patience with those pious religious leaders who marched around looking pure and holy but who had proud, noncaring, holier-than-thou attitudes on the inside.

Such people are around today. You probably know some of them. They like to be admired for their religious activities and knowledge. They set up rules which they think all Christians should follow, and they are critical of others who fail to meet the standards. They pretend to "have it all together" and like to talk about their Christian joy in church meetings.

I won't deny that many of these people are sincere. Often they really want to be good Christians but instead they are immature, proud, and sometimes phony. Frequently they are also confused and hurting inside because they know, down deep, that they really are pretending. Such people can be pretty obnoxious, but maybe we should feel sorry for them.

There is a little church in the eastern United States where the people are real. They worship together on Sunday, are not afraid to share their problems openly, and spend a lot of time doing good and helping people in the neighborhood. In describing his congregation to me, the pastor said, "Our church is not meant to be a museum of perfect saints; it's a rescue place for struggling sinners." I've heard something like that before and to me it's a good picture of what churches *should* be like.

But a lot of churches aren't like that. They are boring, not very tolerant of people who don't fit, and attended by people who apparently have never heard of doubts, failures, sex, drugs, financial pressures, and teenage stress. Members of these churches may talk about accepting, forgiving, encouraging, loving, caring, and helping one another (that's all biblical), but in practice they are using, ignoring, stepping on, rejecting, criticizing, and gossiping about one another. (That's not biblical—but it's common.)

That may sound harsh to you. Certainly not all churches are like this. Nevertheless, the fact that there are at least some hypocrites in almost every church might be of help to you in your thinking.

It also helps to remember that church pews are filled with hurting people—including old people, parents, little kids, and teenagers. These people need to be accepted, respected, and understood. If you treat them with genuine kindness and sincere concern, they might begin to see that pretending isn't necessary—especially in church.

It is helpful to admit that in some ways we are all hypocrites. We all talk about caring but then ignore others in need. We don't like pride, but we secretly look down on others. We may agree that it's important to worship God, but sometimes we forget about Him.

In spite of this, we don't have to be like those religious hypocrites who were criticized by Jesus. They had no desire to change, and they weren't inclined to admit their failures. But we can be different. God is very patient with people—even hypocrites—who confess their sins and really want to do better. He can change you so you won't become one of those adult phonies in church.

Also, it is helpful to conclude that we don't have to throw out our Christianity just because all Christians aren't perfect. One of the great things about Jesus Christ is that He accepts us just as we are. Because of that a lot of misfits, weak people, and even hypocrites get into the church. That's a sign of strength, not an excuse for you to give up on religion.

Philip Yancey has told the story of a teenager who had been raised as a Catholic but refused to go to church because of the nuns. He didn't like their uptightness, their manner, and the way they had treated him in school. Then somebody asked him a question.

"Do you mean to tell me that you're going to let a few little ladies in uniforms keep you from knowing God?"

The same question could be asked of us. "Are we saying that a few uptight hypocrites are enough to keep us from meeting God personally?"

Not long ago I read about a young college student who had become a new Christian. One Sunday he decided to attend church for the first time, but he hadn't thought about dressing up. He arrived barefoot, wearing only "cutoffs" and a T-shirt.

The sanctuary was filled with well-dressed worshipers, and when he reached the front of the church without finding a seat, he squatted down on the floor.

Some of the staid worshipers were aghast, but then they noticed an old man walking down the aisle. He was impeccably dressed, and the people wondered what he would do when he reached that barefooted creature sitting cross-legged on the floor.

To everyone's surprise, the old man lowered himself to the floor and sat there with the visitor during the service. The hypocrites might have scoffed, but most people were touched by an act of kindness that helped a new Christian worship God along with, and in spite of, the other imperfect people in that congregation.

You and I can be honest, too, and worship God even in the midst of hypocrites. After all, we go to school with hypocrites and see them at work, so why shouldn't we get along with them in church—without becoming like them?

Question 3: What can be done about religious pressure? First, you can *expect it*. Jesus never promised us a rose-garden type of Christianity where everything would be beautiful and all problems would melt away like ice on a balmy summer day. On the contrary, He told the disciples to expect problems and rejection because of their beliefs: "... Here on earth," He said, "you will have many trials and sorrows; but cheer up, for I have overcome the world" (John 16:33).

Second, you can *admit it* when religious stress appears. Admit—to God, to yourself, and to others—that you have doubts at times, get angry at God, sometimes resist the Bible's commands (even though they are best for you), struggle when your prayers aren't answered, get bored with Christianity, and are confused about why a loving God permits suffering.

While you're admitting your frustrations, you might also think about the alternatives to what you've got. Suppose your father decided to quit his job because he didn't like the pay, the work, his bosses, or the people he met every day. Before resigning, he might consider the alternatives—especially the fact that he wouldn't have any pay if he quit. The more he considered it, the more he might decide that his present job, with all its frustrations, wasn't so bad after all.

You might conclude the same thing about a relationship with Jesus Christ. The Christian life is frustrating but the alternatives are a lot worse.

A third suggestion about religious pressure is that you can *discuss it*. You should share it with God but it also helps to talk it over with an older believer. Try to find someone who is understanding and not inclined to put you down when you start asking difficult questions. You might be surprised to discover that your parents or a local pastor could help you, although I agree that some adults will be threatened by your questions, so look around. Ask God to show you a good helper.

Finally, *do something about it* if you sense some religious pressure. Try to find answers in books or tapes. Spend some time in prayer and in Bible reading. Try to follow some of the instructions that are taught in Scripture. Reach out to others without condemning. Ask God to bring friends into your life who can help you to face your struggles and live a life pleasing to Christ.

It can be painful and risky to face your questions squarely, to resist the me-religion of our society, and to submit yourself to Jesus Christ. In the midst of the difficulties, however, Jesus promises to give you a life lived to the fullest (John 10:10).

The alternative is to slip either into a phony religion with empty ritual or—even worse—into the futility and meaninglessness of the me-generation.

11

Future Stress:
Finding Some Direction for Life

They have heard it since they were children. Their parents, grandparents, aunts, and uncles have implanted it in their heads. Over and over, adults have been telling them, "High School is the best time of your life." A depressing thought considering how unhappy most students are. Seniors are especially unhappy because of the enormous amount of academic pressure.

Kim Fridkin, the student who wrote these words, was a high school senior who did a survey on teenage stress as part of a class project. I don't suppose the survey was very scientific—it covered only one school—but it is interesting to read her conclusions. I am grateful to Kim for letting me quote from this fascinating article which was written for the student paper. The name of the high school has been taken out but, apart from that, this is what she wrote:

> *Students feel pressure because of their parents.* Many of the students' parents encourage them to study often. The parents believe a successful student is one who studies diligently and consistently.... The students feel that grades are very important for them to be a success. A lot of students believe if they are unsuccessful, their parents will be unhappy with them....
>
> *Students feel pressure from their peers.* It is apparent that cheating runs rampant in our high school. This fact was unfortunately confirmed in the survey. Eighty-four percent of the students surveyed have cheated at least once on a test. Forty-four have cheated from five to ten times, and 18 percent have cheated "too many times to count." Possibly the reason for these high results is peer pressure. Ours is a highly competitive school with grades being highly important to a great number of students.
>
> When a student knows his friend is cheating and will get a good grade, he wants to do the same. He knows grades are important, and because cheating almost always goes unnoticed, he feels no risk. Since everyone is cheating, he wants to do it too. The student can rationalize, and his act will seem harmless. He may think to himself, "Everyone cheats; if I don't cheat, I'll be the only one with a lousy grade. I want a good grade, so I'll cheat too." Only students with high moral standards can resist the temptation to cheat. Unfortunately, results indicate high morals are not in great abundance at our school. In addition, many students feel a lot of pressure about getting into college. Forty-six percent of the seniors feel "a lot of" pressure about getting into college. Thirty-six percent of the seniors feel "too much" pressure. Sixteen percent of the seniors admitted to feeling "some" pressure. This pressure probably comes from their peers....

Finally, and most significantly, *students put pressure on themselves.* . . . Self-imposed pressure becomes evident when students are asked what they would do if they did not get into the school of their choice. The results were humorous, yet also alarming. Fifty-two percent of the students said they would be upset, but would apply to their second choice school and perhaps transfer. Eighteen percent said they would cry and 30 percent stated that they would commit suicide. Of course, this response is "tongue in cheek," yet the pressure of getting into college comes distinctly through in this humorous response. Many students set goals for themselves and throughout high school they strive to obtain their goals. The realization of their success or failure becomes evident in their senior year and pressure results. The amount of pressure the seniors put on themselves becomes evident with worry about grades. Eight percent said, "sometimes," 60 percent said "most of the time," and 32 percent said they worried about grades "all the time." . . .

High school is not the best time for many. They feel an enormous amount of academic pressure, perhaps too much. Has school changed so much in the past twenty years, or is it that parents, grandparents, aunts, and uncles have chosen to repress the unpleasant pressure of their high school life?

I took the time to share this student's article because it clearly shows the stresses that many high schoolers face as they think about the future. There is pressure from parents who want their offspring to get good grades and pressure from peers who encourage cheating. Pressure from inside teenagers themselves comes as they struggle to do well academically, to get accepted by a college, to be successful, to avoid failure, and to handle moral struggles about whether or not they should cheat.

A lot of this pressure reduces to one big question: *How do I face the future?*

To answer this we must think about four significant questions: *Who am I? Where am I going? How do I make decisions about the future? What can I do now to get ready for the future?*

Identity: The Question of "Who Am I?"

Let me tell you about a psychiatrist named William Glasser. He's written several books and reached some interesting conclusions, partly because of his work with teenagers in California.

According to Dr. Glasser, all human beings have one basic need. He calls this the need for identity—"the need to feel that each of us is somehow separate and distinctive from every other living being on the face of this earth and that no other person thinks, looks, acts, and talks exactly as we do." This is a need to be unique, to be someone special.

I used to have a young psychologist working for me. He was a capable and dedicated worker, but after a couple of years he got tired of being known as "Gary's assistant." Maybe you've felt the same way when people have forgotten your name and can only remember that you are "Joe's boy," "Wendy's sister," or "Karen's cousin." Most of us would prefer to be known by name and to be recognized for who we are and what we can do.

This desire to be unique is healthy, but it can create problems. It can put us in conflict with parents and other significant people who don't understand why we want to be so different. It can lead to rebellion and even lawbreaking as some young people try to step out on their own. It can cause younger teenagers to almost worship rock stars and other heroes who appear to live unique and glamorous lives. The need for identity also causes teens to latch onto hairstyles, beliefs, attitudes, personal habits, and slang that set them apart from the more staid (that means "older") members of the society.

Of course nobody wants to be too different because people might then reject us and think we are odd. The teenager, therefore, has a big struggle. He or she wants to develop a unique identity without looking like a "kooky" social misfit.

This struggle is what some people have called the *identity crisis*. It is a struggle to discover who you are and where you fit in the world. It's a time in life that can leave you with a lot of confusion.

I wish I could tell you that there's a fast, convenient way out of this identity struggle, but there isn't. The physical and psychological changes taking place in you, the confusing changes that are shaking our society, and the difficulty of knowing where and how you fit in all combine to make this a difficult period of life.

All is not hopeless, however. Most people do "find themselves," and there are some things you can do to make this easier. *Find yourself through your roots.* If you cut yourself off from family and friends you can be terribly lonely and confused. Why not start, instead, by recognizing where you are now, even if you don't want to stay there. Think about the fact that you are

- a member of the _____ family,
- a resident of _____,
- age _____,
- a part of the _____ race,
- descended from people who come from _____,
- probably of lower-, middle-, or upper- (choose one) class background,
- involved in the _____ church,
- a friend of _____,
- interested in _____,
- really good at doing _____, and
- thinking about a career in _____.

Once you get a picture of where you are now, you have a clearer base from which to move on to the next step.
Find yourself through your contacts with others. Dr. Glasser believes that we never find ourselves until we know that somewhere

out in the world there is at least one person who loves us just as we are.

Sometimes such a person is hard to find. As they search, many teenagers try to find acceptance by getting involved with people who are on drugs or in criminal gangs. Others join cliques which cruelly exclude people who are different, and some jump into bed at every opportunity, hoping to find love or at least acceptance in a sexual relationship.

I don't know if you've ever read J. D. Salinger's novel *The Catcher in the Rye*. While it uses a lot of gutter language, the novel makes a strong statement. It vividly tells the story of a six-teen-year-old named Holden Caulfield who tries to find himself by going into the underground side of New York. When the book ends, Holden is as confused as he was when he started. He's met a lot of people and had a lot of experiences, but he still hasn't been accepted or really loved by anyone.

When you struggle like this, let me remind you that God accepts you—just as you are and without any hesitation or strings attached. That can be pretty comforting, especially the next time you feel alone.

If you think about it, there probably are some human beings who accept you as well. If not, ask God to lead you to such a person or persons. Don't try to force other people into liking you. Be yourself, be friendly, and be a caring person. In time, others will notice and respond with kindness and acceptance.

Find yourself through your religion. I wonder if the people who reject God ever really solve the Who am I? problem.

God thinks that we are valuable people. He created us, put us in families, gave us abilities and interests, helped each of us develop a personality, and sent His Son, Jesus, to pay for our sins and to forgive us whenever we do something wrong.

According to Dr. Glasser, we don't solve the identity problem until we feel that we are worthwhile human beings. You might question your value and others may wonder if you are worth much, but God (who knows you better than you know yourself) believes you are valuable—even when you fail, sin, rebel against Him, or do stupid things. If we never amount to anything worthwhile, God still says we are valuable individuals.

That can give us a real anchor of stability in a confusing world. *Find yourself through your successes.* Please let me mention Dr. Glasser one more time. He thinks that as we go through life we begin to think of ourselves as being successful or as being a failure. If you consider yourself a failure, then life is lonely, confusing, anxious, and depressing. If you think of yourself as a success, you are likely to be more content and satisfied with life.

If I asked you what it means to be successful you might talk about being a good athlete or student, being liked, or having money and prestige. Surprisingly, that's not the Bible's view of success.

Two brothers once came to Jesus, along with their mother, and asked if they could please have an important place in heaven.

"You're wanting to be successful by being important," Jesus said, and that is certainly society's definition of success.

Then Jesus made a mind-boggling statement: "If you want to be right at the top, you must serve like a slave" (Matthew 20:27). In God's view, the successful person is the one who cares about others.

Besides being a radical idea, this is encouraging. We can all be successful in God's eyes because we can all find ways to help others.

Even before she won the Nobel Prize, Mother Teresa was someone whom I greatly admired. She is a nun who has given her life to help the poor and starving people of India. That lady is successful and has found her identity in life. She found it by helping others.

Find yourself through your vocation. Unless you are independently wealthy (and maybe even then), you probably are expecting to work for the rest of your life. A lot of people find themselves when they finally choose a vocation.

Regrettably, that is one of the greatest stresses facing teenagers, especially when they get to be high school juniors and seniors. That gets us to the next important question about the future.

Direction: The Question of "Where Am I Going?"

When I was a student there, Westdale High School had about 1,700 students but there was only one guidance counselor. His name was Mr. Bell—an understanding and friendly man—but he was a part-time teacher who obviously didn't have much time for helping students plan their careers. I think I saw him twice during my years in high school.

Total time: about thirty minutes.

Total expectation on my part: high.

Total help: none!

I hope it's better in your school, but if it isn't, maybe you can take some comfort in the story of Abraham. He lived in a remote country and probably never went to high school. I doubt that he had much choice about his vocation, and it must have come as a surprise when, one day, God told him to move. Abraham was seventy-five and perhaps ready to retire. To make matters worse, God didn't say where Abraham was supposed to go, but he obeyed and moved even though he didn't know where he was headed.

Most of life is like that. We can make plans for the future, but we never know for sure what will happen in the years ahead. God doesn't give us clear blueprints for life in advance. If we're like most people, we'll change jobs several times before we retire, and some of us will change our careers at least once or twice.

How, then, can we possibly plan for the future—with or without a guidance counselor? The answer, I suggest, is to keep your options open so you can be free to make changes as you move along through life.

My friend Steve decided in high school that he wanted to be a doctor. That's a noble goal. A lot of people want to be physicians, but few get there.

Steve didn't! He started toward medical school but did poorly in chemistry and discovered that his grades were too low to get accepted at the university of his choice. This was a crushing blow, but he started looking for a second choice. He considered veterinary medicine, counseling, physical therapy, and some other helping professions. Eventually he went to college and seminary, and now he's a very successful hospital chaplain. He likes his job and knows that he found it by keeping an open mind. He's not a doctor, but because he was able to consider several other career choices, he is doing what he most wanted to do anyway—giving help to people who are hurting and in need.

Let me suggest that, in planning for your future, you take the time to write out your answers to the following questions. Keep the paper in a drawer someplace so you can add to it as you think more about these questions later.

- What are my major interests?
- What are some more minor interests?
- What do I do well? (This concerns your abilities.)
- What would I like to be doing in five years, ten years, fifty years? (This concerns your goals.)
- How can I get to where I want to be? (Try to think of some specific things to do.)
- Given my interests, abilities, and goals, what jobs are available?
- What do I know about these jobs? (What is the pay? What are the hours? What is the future for the occupation? You can get answers to these questions by visiting the library or talking to people who are in these jobs.)
- How do I get into these jobs? (What training do you need? How do you get it? Is it expensive?)

It is probable that you will change your mind several times during the next few years, so it can be helpful to keep collecting information. If you go to college, try to take a variety of subjects so you can see what you like and dislike.

This was important to a student who recently sent me a letter from Nigeria.

"I thought I wanted to be a psychologist," he wrote, "but I took a psychology course and hated it!" You might have a similar experience with psychology or some other subject. If so, you've learned something about yourself and about a possible area of work. This can prevent a lot of grief later.

Decisions: The Question of "How Do I Make Choices?"

When I was a teenager, I decided that it would be great to visit Australia. I'm not sure why I wanted this, except for the fact that Australia is far away and has always seemed to be a fascinating country.

Not long ago I finally made the trip—and loved it. I met a lot of interesting people but was especially impressed by a conversation with a man who works in a youth organization.

"A lot of the kids here don't have any hope," he said. "Many of them think that the world will blow up within the next few years, so they've concluded that they should live it up now while there's still time."

I'm beginning to think that such a view isn't limited to Australia—or even to the late twentieth century. Jesus talked about people who decided that they would "eat, drink, and be merry" since they might be dead tomorrow.

The problem with this way of thinking is that we might *not* be dead tomorrow. We may enjoy ourselves now, but without planning and preparation the years ahead could be pretty bleak.

For the Christian (and probably for some non-Christians as well) there is the added issue of wanting to know God's leading for the future. In Abraham's day, God spoke through dreams, visions, angels, and voices from heaven, but that does not happen anymore. So how do we determine God's will for our lives?

We must want it. For a lot of us, that's the biggest hurdle. Somehow we've got the idea that whenever we let God lead, He'll make life miserable. Perhaps He'll lead us to a boring missionary job, take away all our fun, and show that He wants us to marry somebody who is ugly. Relax! There isn't even a hint of this in the Bible. God's not a sadist who delights in making our lives miserable. He wants what is best for us.

We must expect it. God doesn't play hide-and-seek with His will for us. He doesn't always give us the full picture right away, but He has promised to lead us if we really want Him to do so (*see* Psalms 32:8; Proverbs 3:5, 6).

I know a lady whose husband died while they were in Africa. She was plunged into deep grief and felt very lonely, being so far away from home.

One very dark, tropical night an African neighbor came to her door for some reason and then turned to go home. He was carrying a small kerosene lantern with a smoky chimney. To say the least, it wasn't very bright, and the lady expressed some concern about its usefulness.

"That little lamp doesn't give much light, does it?"

"No," the visitor replied. "It doesn't. But it shines as far as I can step."

God leads us like that. He doesn't always give us a high-powered searchlight to penetrate the darkness way ahead. But He always lights the way at least for the immediate future—which is only as far as we can step.

We must seek it. God never expects us to turn off our brains when we are looking for His will and making decisions about the future. For many years I wanted to be a singer. Having been born in the same year as Elvis Presley and Pat Boone (maybe you can figure out my age), I wanted to follow in their musical footsteps.

There has always been one little hitch in this plan, however: I can't sing very well, and I don't know how to play any instruments—not even a guitar. Now it doesn't take a collection of psychological tests for me to know that a musical career is not for me. I concluded that with my God-given brain.

Several paragraphs back, I suggested that you answer some questions about your interests, abilities, and goals. That's using your brain to seek God's guidance.

You can also ask the guidance counselor to give you some tests. These won't point you to exact jobs but they can help to narrow your choices. The opinions and advice of people who know you well can help (your parents might be especially helpful here), and you can also learn from your experiences and opportunities. If your application to law school gets rejected, then, at least for now, you know that this is not the direction in which you should go. The opportunity isn't there.

And don't overlook the help that comes from the Bible— God's Word. This Book won't tell you who to marry or where to work, but it can give you some good guidance as you make specific decisions.

We must cool it.   Some people get very uptight over decisions in life. If we want, expect, and are seeking God's leading, however, we can relax, knowing that He *will* guide. Even if we make a mistake, it's unlikely that life will end or that the earth will explode. We'll simply have to pick ourselves up, learn from our mistakes, and keep going. Millions have done that before. You can do it too!

Conclusion: The Question of "What Can I Do Now?"

As you will remember, this chapter began with some quotations from a high school newspaper. The writer mentioned that a lot of students feel pressure from parents, other people, and themselves, especially when it comes time to make decisions about the future.

You don't have to sit around feeling pressure, however. There are some things you can do right now.

You can try to appreciate the present. That statement may

seem strange when we are thinking about planning ahead, but you've probably seen some people who seem to be always thinking about the future. They are so busy looking forward to life when they graduate, when they start working, when they leave home, or when they get married, that they miss many pleasant experiences right now. Think about it. What can you appreciate about the present?

Then you can learn to plan ahead. Even while we enjoy the present, it still makes sense to plan for the future. Don't be like those Australian kids (and many North American and European kids) who have given up. They are likely to be sorry later.

You can decide what action can be taken now. What can you do today or this week to reduce some of your stresses and to move toward your future goals? You can learn, for example, to be an employee, now. Part-time jobs can be good experiences. They can teach you to be on time, to be patient (especially when the boss isn't), to be tolerant, and to be responsible. They also will show you that life in the working world isn't always easy, fair, or fun.

Before getting to high school, I worked for several years in a drugstore—dusting shelves and delivering prescriptions. Later I went to work part-time at Eaton's—a large department store where I sold socks, then shoes (was that a promotion?), and later I worked in the cash office. The latter especially was a responsible job that taught me a lot about money. (It also taught me to be careful not to lean on the burglar alarm. I did this once accidentally and discovered that it is possible for one teenager to send a six-floor department store and local police department into a panic!)

Finally, you can try to help others—every day if possible. This can keep you from becoming self-centered and can even take off some of the pressure that comes from thinking too much about the future.

12

Teen Stress: Guidelines for Managing Pressure

Have you ever thought about leaving home?

I'm not talking about running away. Thousands of teenagers decide to do this every year when the pressures get too great, and usually the results are devastating for both the teens and the worried family that is left behind.

What I'm thinking about here, however, is leaving home to go to college, to join the military, to get married, or just to move into your own apartment across town.

Unlike some societies that have elaborate ceremonies to mark a young person's move into adulthood, we have nothing. There is no right time or age to go out on your own. Young adults want to be independent, but it can be hard to leave—and expensive. As they leave, kids often feel anxious, sad, lonely, and sometimes guilty—but they also want the freedom of being on their own.

It isn't easy for parents either. Most of them have no desire to cling too long and most don't want to push their grown children out, but parents often feel a reluctance to let go, especially when the youngest or only child wants to move out.

I was eighteen when I left for the first time, but it was only for a summer. Later I went away to college, but it was possible to get home on weekends. When I was in my early twenties, however, I went to Europe—with a one-way ticket and no money to get back. It was hard to go but my family and I all needed the sharp break—and we have since grown closer together because of it.

By now you realize, I'm sure, that stresses don't stop when you leave adolescence. Leaving home is stressful, starting college can be stressful. Launching your career, marriage, or family can each be exciting—and stressful. It continues this way all through your life.

Like teenagers, some adults handle pressure well, others barely survive, and some buckle under. But there are some general guidelines that can help you handle pressure now and in the future. We might call them the ten commandments for stress management. You've seen them scattered in the preceding pages, but now let's pull them together into a formula that could help you in handling any stresses—even those that haven't yet been mentioned.

1. Admit It

This isn't always as easy as it might seem. Many people think that admitting a problem is a sign of weakness, even though it's really a sign of strength. Probably you know people who hope that if they don't face a problem it will go away—at least for a while. I've known girls who handle a pregnancy that way. They try to ignore it, but of course it can't be ignored forever—even with a tight girdle and baggy clothes. The sooner a stressful problem is faced, the better.

Sometimes, however, we don't even realize that we are under stress until our bodies start to give us some clues. When we are unusually tired, overly critical, anxious, irritable (more than usual), easily discouraged, unable to concentrate (especially on schoolwork), losing our appetites, unable to sleep, prone to have accidents, or bothered by a number of physical symptoms—these all can signal stress. They are ways in which our bodies cry "Ouch! Do something!"

When you have physical symptoms it's always wise to see a doctor, but, especially when there is nothing physically wrong, you can also ask, *What's bothering me?* Often some friend or concerned adult can help you decide.

As you admit that the stress exists, don't be afraid of tears and please don't buy into these two self-defeating ways of thinking: *I'm the only one to have this stress* or *I'll never be able to change.* In most cases these statements are not true and believing them can do a lot to increase your pressure.

2. Pray About It

Sometimes we think of prayer as a last resort, but it should be a first line of defense against the stresses of life.

God, who created us, also understands. He has promised to stick with us, to guide us, and to give us the ability to resist temptation.

In praying, remember that God knows what is best for us— and what is best isn't always what we want. God isn't a genie who jumps whenever we snap our fingers and gives us exactly what we request. If He was like that, God would be in a real bind when two guys each prayed for a date on the same night with the same girl or when members of two opposing football teams each prayed for victory.

Please don't get me wrong. I do believe that we can pray even over the tiniest things in life—like finding a parking place or a washroom when we need one or both of these. But it seems to me that our chief requests should be for wisdom in ourselves and others, for God's protection and guidance, and for a willingness to accept God's plans for us without bitterness, even when we might have wanted something else.

Many years ago there was a Catholic monk in France named Brother Lawrence. He wasn't especially brilliant or influential while he lived, and his job—working in the kitchen of the monastery—couldn't have been very exciting. But Brother Lawrence learned to carry on continual conversations with God. Here were friends who communicated regularly. I suspect that God molded the monk's thinking and he, in turn, was clearly "in tune" with God's desires.

I think this is a good example for us. Brother Lawrence called it "practicing the presence of God." It involved the desire and effort to think about God often during the day and to send up little prayers all the time, and not just when big crises arrived. Brother Lawrence knew something about handling stress.

3. Analyze It

Since this book is written by a psychologist, you probably assumed that I'd talk about *analysis* sooner or later.

But I'm not suggesting anything complicated. I'm not indicating that you should try to "psychoanalyze yourself." (That, by the way, is something which can't be done without help.)

Instead, when stresses come along I would encourage you to take inventory. Just before tax time, most store owners have their employees count the stock to see what is on the shelves and what is missing. In a sense that's what we do when we take stock of our current stress. Ask yourself:

- What specific things are pulling me under stress?
- What am I doing to cope with my stress?
- What strengths do I have for dealing with the stress?
- What weakness will I have to overcome?

- What things can I do now to deal with the stressful situation? (Be specific.)
- What things could be done at a later time?

It helps if you can write answers to these questions on paper. Then you have a plan of action in front of you—in black and white.

4. Look At It

Ask yourself, *Is there more than one way to look at the stress or problems I'm facing?*

I once counseled with a girl who had been in all kinds of trouble with the police. During one of our counseling sessions I was called from the room, and when I returned Carol was seated with her back to the door looking pretty dejected. Without thinking, I placed my hand gently on her shoulder. It was meant to be a gesture of support—a way to say "I care."

But Carol didn't see it that way.

In a flash she leapt to her feet, fists swinging, and almost hit me right in the face.

Suddenly she stopped herself.

"Don't ever touch me!" she blurted out. "I'm used to swinging first and asking questions later."

Carol had learned to see the world as a hostile place. Even a slight touch on the shoulder had been interpreted as something threatening.

When we look at a problem, we see it from our own viewpoint, and we need to remember that others may see it differently.

Recently I was listening to a radio commentator describe a football game between his favorite team and Purdue University. When Purdue got a touchdown the commentator indicated that this was "unfortunate." As a Purdue graduate, I didn't agree. Clearly the commentator and I saw the situation differently.

When you are under stress ask yourself if there is another way of looking at the problem. Perhaps what seems so bad might not be as bad after all. (Or, it could be worse!)

You might also try asking yourself, *What if the worst thing imaginable happens?* Probably it won't, but even if your worst fears do come to pass the results may not be as terrible as you think.

5. Decide What You Will Do About It

We can spend hours thinking about a problem, but eventually we have to take some action.

Reducing the complexity of your life is one obvious, but sometimes forgotten, way of cutting down the stress. Sometimes we have too much to do and must decide to drop some activities. Even the shape your room is in can help. Loud music, flashing lights, bright posters and wallpaper, or piles of junk can all create distractions and make it harder to face the stresses.

Planning ahead can also be helpful since this takes off some of the time pressures.

Then, of course, it sometimes is necessary to change yourself, to talk over a problem with someone, or even to leave a stress situation for a while.

If you are under stress and can't think of anything to do, talk to someone who can help you make some decisions.

6. Avoid Self-Defeatist Reactions to It

Everybody has heard that it is wise to count to ten before you blow up when something makes you mad. This isn't a bad idea. Sometimes the ten-second delay, while you count, is enough to calm you down so you don't say something that you will regret later.

Many times when we are under pressure, and especially when we're angry, we do things that are meant to hurt others but we really harm ourselves more. There really are people who commit suicide to "get even" with somebody, although this certainly is the height of self-defeat—and stupidity. The same thing is happening when a teenager deliberately does poorly in school, gets pregnant, or runs away in an attempt to hurt parents. The parents probably will suffer but it is likely that, in the end, the teen will suffer more. If you quit your job to get revenge on your boss, you may find that he or she recovers quickly and hires someone else, leaving you with no paycheck.

I knew a man who actually got mad at a bus driver and demanded to be let off so he could walk home defiantly, in protest—and in the heat. I wonder what he thought that would accomplish? It wasn't the bus driver who got the sore feet!

Let me suggest that you learn to think through the consequences before you act. This isn't always easy, of course, but it is worth the effort. Ask yourself, *Do I really want to send the letter I wrote, to stay away from the party, to say what I'm thinking, to leave home, to take the drug—or to do whatever else I'm pondering?*

Often, I suspect, you'll decide that it's better, in the long run, to face a problem in a more realistic way instead of doing something that you will be sorry for later.

7. Back Away From It

Sometimes I'm invited to talk to businessmen, housewives, pastors, and college students about their stresses. Usually I tell them to slow down for a while and think about their whole lives. Too often these people are busy, busy, busy. They run from one activity to another, and then wonder why they feel so tired and pressured.

Maybe some teens need the same message: Are you getting enough sleep and physical exercise? Is your diet well balanced and not overloaded with "junk foods"? Are you avoiding alcohol and drugs? Are you overly involved in athletics, work, study, music, a hobby, or some other activity that is consuming too much of your time?

It really impresses me that Jesus didn't get overwhelmed by the pressures of His life. If you read Mark 1, you will discover that He was busy. After what seems to have been a particularly hectic day, for example, Jesus went to have dinner at the home of Peter, one of the disciples. The neighbors found out about this, and by sunset the street was filled with a huge crowd of people, many of whom had come for healing. Jesus must have worked late into the night, but "the next morning he was up long before daybreak and went out alone into the wilderness to pray" (Mark 1:35). Clearly He talked to His Father in heaven, but while He was alone might Jesus also have thought about the day and asked God to give Him wisdom to keep everything in balance?

Probably we can spend too much time alone. That can be unhealthy. It is equally unhealthy, however, to rush through the teen years without taking frequent breaks to be alone with God and with yourself. Backing away like this can do wonders to clear your thinking and let you make some decisions about how you can change your life to make it less stressful.

8. Talk About It

I once counseled with a girl named Debbie who loved to talk about her problems. She talked to her counselor (me), her pastor, her teachers, her parents, her neighbors, to the people she worked with, and to the other kids at school. Before long, people cringed whenever they saw her coming. They had problems of their own and didn't want to listen to Debbie's endless tales of woe.

You've probably met people like this. So, in order to avoid burdening others, as Debbie did, you may have decided to never say anything about your pressures.

Too little talking, however, can also be harmful—perhaps

even worse than saying too much. Keeping our concerns and stresses bottled up inside only increases the pressure and makes matters worse. When we are under stress, we sometimes feel confused, overwhelmed, and not sure what to do. At such times it makes sense to talk things over with someone else.

It isn't necessary to talk incessantly about our stresses or to discuss them with a lot of people. Think of some person who is understanding and who isn't likely to tell others about your problem after you have talked. You might want to talk to someone your own age. Such a person could be very understanding, even though he or she might not have much to offer in the way of practical suggestions. An older person will have a different perspective, more experience, and more wisdom, but older people don't always understand completely. Before you talk in detail, therefore, try out more than one helper until you find someone who can truly help.

I am always reminding myself that God put us in the midst of people. Unlike Debbie, whenever I get under stress I tend to withdraw. This can be overdone and isn't healthy. It is much better to accept the encouragement and support of other people. It is no mark of superiority to struggle alone.

9. Learn From It

I teach at a school where most students are in their mid-twenties. Our courses run for about ten weeks and it is interesting to see how the students handle the school pressures. They start the first week enthusiastically, coast along until midterm exams, coast a little more, and then work like crazy during the last two weeks. After finishing their work, almost in a state of exhaustion, some of them decide that they have learned their lesson.

"Next time it will be different," some of them have said, but they don't seem to learn. Next time it's the same old pressures all over again.

This probably sounds familiar. We want to learn from our mistakes but we often don't.

Perhaps, however, you can learn from your stresses. Whenever they come and go, ask yourself, *Did I learn anything from this? How can I handle things better next time?*

As you think about this, you might profit from reading some words written by the Apostle Paul when he was in jail. The God who helped him can help you to reach the same conclusions:

> ... I have learned how to get along happily whether I have much or little. I know how to live on almost nothing or with everything. I have learned the secret of content-ment in every situation, whether it be a full stomach or hunger, plenty or want; for I can do everything God asks me to with the help of Christ who gives me the strength and power.
>
> Philippians 4:11–13

10. Reach Out From It

One of my friends edits a magazine for single adults. When we last met, he told me some things about the articles that people send in hoping to have printed.

"Almost all of them are about how we can handle our own problems," he said. "They talk about such things as handling money, dealing with anxiety, learning to study, and raising kids."

Then my friend added an interesting but sad comment. "These writers are caught up in the me-first way of thinking. Nobody has written an article about helping others."

Apparently these writers haven't realized that one of the most powerful ways of helping ourselves is to help others.

In chapter 4 I mentioned Alcoholics Anonymous. It's an orga-nization in which people who have a drinking problem spend time helping one another to stop drinking. Everybody in AA helps and everybody benefits. Something similar happens in Alateen—the organization of teenagers who help each other live in homes where there is an alcoholic parent. If you want to find an Alateen group near you, look in the phone book under Alcoholics Anonymous, call the number, and ask whoever answers to tell you about Alateen.

What these people have discovered was taught in the Bible centuries ago. We all have a responsibility to be helpful, caring people.

It's overly simple, perhaps, but maybe the best way to end this book is to remind you that you are not alone in facing stress. God will help you, others can help you, and you can do some things yourself. But one of the best ways to cope is to ask God to help you care for others.

When you reach out, your own stresses come into clearer perspective and often begin to fade. That's a healthy way to give yourself a break and to effectively handle the pressures of life.

A Final Word

Terry Fox (I'm using a real name now) was a hero!

As a teenager he was active in athletics and well liked by his friends at the high school he attended in western Canada. In those days nobody ever dreamed that Terry would attract world-wide attention as a very young man.

It began when the doctors discovered that Terry had cancer. That can be bad news for anybody, but imagine how this athletic teenager felt when he had to have his cancerous leg cut off. Then came more bad news: The cancer still hadn't been stopped.

I might have given up at that point! Maybe you would have quit too. But Terry got the idea that he could still do something with his life. He decided to run across Canada, from coast to coast, encouraging people to give money for cancer research.

It was painful, running on his artificial leg, but Terry kept

going. He started on the shores of the Atlantic and his goal was
the Pacific Coast.

He never made it!

Four and a half months after he began, and 3,300 miles from
the place where he had started, Terry Fox had to quit. The
cancer had spread too far; he couldn't continue. When they took
him to the hospital, Terry cried—and so did a lot of other people.

The next day his picture was in every newspaper in Canada.
He had raised $24 million for cancer research. The government
presented him with the Order of Canada medal—the highest civilian award that country can give. It was announced that the
country planned to issue a stamp bearing Terry's picture—even
though the Canadian post office had never before honored a living civilian in this way.

Before the stamp was printed, Terry died. All over the nation
people mourned and flags fluttered at half-staff. Terry was only
twenty-two—not much beyond the teen years. He had faced
more stress than many of us will ever see, and he had risen above
it.

This book was written with the hope that you too can learn to
handle stresses and rise above them. You and I might never become heroes like Terry Fox, but with God's help we can become
better people in spite of our pressures.

*   *   *

Anybody who has ever written a book report or term paper
knows that writing can be slow, boring, and sometimes stressful
work. It can also be fun, and I hope you could tell that I enjoyed
writing these pages.

From the start, though, I was a little worried about whether a
middle-aged guy like me could really say something to help people like you who are a lot younger. So when the book was fin-
ished I showed it to a few friends, including some teens. They
made many helpful suggestions, and I want to mention their
names in print. I didn't accept all of their ideas (if you didn't like

the book, blame me, not them), but I really appreciated their help.

So, thank you Lynn Collins, Jan Collins, Julie Collins (they're my relatives), Chris Cone, Dave Currie, Jeff Deckert, Terry Fuchs, Victor Oliver, Ann Stanger, Carol Thor, and Ty Willems. Cheryl Zminda and Lenore Scherrer typed the manuscript (which meant they had to read my handwriting), and the kids at Arlington Heights Free Church listened more or less patiently while I gave out all of these ideas in a series of Sunday morning talks. Thank you!

Before I say good-bye, let me also thank you, my readers, for letting me share my thoughts with you. I sincerely hope that God will use these ideas to help you become the kind of person that He really wants you to be—in spite of (and maybe because of) your pressures.

Suggested Reading List

Allen, Loyd V. *Drug Abuse: What Can We Do?* Ventura, Calif.: Regal Books, 1981.

Aseltine, Gwen Pamenter. *Honest Answers About Dating and Sex.* Old Tappan, N.J.: Fleming H. Revell Company, 1982.

Dobbert, John. *If Being a Christian Is So Great, Why Do I Have the Blahs?* Ventura, Calif.: Regal Books, 1980.

Dobbert, John, and Dobbert, Dawn. *Dear Dawn, Dear Dad.* Old Tappan, N.J.: Fleming H. Revell Company, 1980.

Dobson, James. *Preparing for Adolescence.* Santa Ana, Calif.: Vision House Pubs., 1978.

Hartley, Fred. *Update: A New Approach to Christian Dating.* Old Tappan, N.J.: Fleming H. Revell Company, 1977, 1982.

Hartley, Fred. *Dare to Be Different: Dealing With Peer Pressure.* Old Tappan, N.J.: Fleming H. Revell Company, 1980.

Hartley, Fred. *Growing Pains: First Aid for Teenagers.* Old Tappan, N.J.: Fleming H. Revell Company, 1981

Kesler, Jay. *The Strong Weak People.* Wheaton, Ill.: Victor Books, 1976.

Kesler, Jay. *Growing Places.* Old Tappan, N.J.: Fleming H. Revell Company, 1978.

Little, Paul. *Know Why You Believe.* Downers Grove, Ill.: Inter-Varsity Press, 1967.

Pinnock, Clark. *Set Forth Your Case.* Chicago: Moody Press, 1967.

Stafford, Tim. *A Love Story: Questions and Answers on Sex.* Grand Rapids: The Zondervan Corporation, 1977.

Stafford, Tim. *The Trouble with Parents.* Grand Rapids: The Zondervan Corporation, 1978.

Wood, Barry. *Questions Teenagers Ask About Dating and Sex.* Old Tappan, N.J.: Fleming H. Revell Company, 1981.

Yancey, Philip, and Stafford, Tim. *The Unhappy Secrets of the Christian Life.* Grand Rapids: The Zondervan Corporation, 1979.

Index

GIVE ME A BREAK: Study Guide

Introduction

Stress has become a major concern in recent years. According to a report from the American Medical Association, "fifty percent of all visits by patients to physicians involve stress. As a health problem, that makes stress more common than the common cold."

Perhaps one of the most stressful times in life comes during the teenage years. The pressures of these years are well-known: conflicts with parents, pressures from peers and teachers, struggles over values and beliefs, intense feelings of insecurity and discouragement, low self-esteem, worries about the future, preoccupation with dating and sex, and a host of others.

Give Me a Break: The How-to-Handle-Pressure Book for Teens was written as a guidebook to help teenagers understand and deal with the problem of stress. The book is addressed to teenage readers, but its information can be helpful to parents, teachers, and others who have contact with young people as they move into adulthood.

As a supplement to *Give Me a Break,* this growthbook-study guide has been prepared to help teenagers and their leaders understand and cope more effectively with the pressures of life. Each of the following chapters (a) gives a summary of the content in *Give Me a Break,* (b) suggests a practical and personal "growth project" to help teens better understand and face the stress issue described in the book, (c) gives some questions for group discussion or individual consideration, and (d) ends with a concluding thought.

Readers can work through this growthbook alone or with others in a group. Teachers or youth leaders may want to use this book as the basis for a course, Sunday school class, or group discussion series on teenage stress.

Encourage the teens to read the appropriate chapter in *Give Me a Break* before the class or group meeting. When the group convenes, give a summary of the chapter, introduce the "growth project" and allow time for it to be completed, ask students to give their responses to the "questions for thought and discussion," and end with any conclusion that you as the group leader may wish to make.

If the group is large, you may want to have the participants divide into small groups of three or four people who can share their responses to the "growth projects" and discuss the questions. Encourage the teenagers to discuss how this material applies to their lives, but do not pressure people to talk if they don't wish to do so. Also, do not encourage the detailed sharing of anything that could be embarrassing or harmful.

As you read through this growthbook, remember that the teenager is not odd or unusual because he or she encounters stress. Everybody has stress and although teenage stress is in some respects unique, in other respects it is similar to the stresses that all people face throughout life. And teenage stress, while sometimes intense, is also stress that can be handled.

Hope, then, is the theme that pervades this book and should permeate any group which reads *Give Me a Break,* and uses this growthbook.

1

Making the Best of Stress

- What is the meaning of *stress*?
- How does it affect teenagers?
- How do teens respond to the pressures of life?
- How can stress be handled more effectively?

Give Me a Break was written to answer questions such as these. The first chapter begins with some comments about teenage suicide and moves quickly to define the meaning of *stress*.

Chapter 1 then shows that stress can come from three sources: our relationships with others, frustrating circumstances, and inner turmoil.

In seeking to reduce the pressure that these stressors bring, people often turn to one or more of ten possible reactions to stress. These are outlined in this chapter: the dreamer reaction, the complainer reaction, the brooder reaction, the joker reaction, the charmer reaction, the explainer reaction, the avoider reaction, the actor reaction, the tackler reaction, and the believer reaction.

The chapter ends with a reminder that each of us is unique—and we all can learn to understand and handle stress more effectively.

Growth Projects

At times, we all use most of the ten stress reactions mentioned above. It helps to admit that, but there also can be value in trying to understand which of the ten reactions we use most often.

The following exercise is designed to make you aware of how you respond to stress.

On the questionnaire on the next page, indicate how you think you handle stress. In each of the ten reactions, circle the number that applies to you. There are no right or wrong answers. If you circle one of the lower numbers (1, 2, 3) this means that you show the reaction very seldom. If you circle one of the higher numbers, you are indicating that this is one of your most frequent reactions to stress.

If you can't remember what each of these "reactions" is, please go back to Chapter 1 to refresh your memory.

Now find a friend who knows you well and ask how he or she thinks you handle stress. Have your friend circle the most appropriate number

HOW I HANDLE STRESS

Type of Reaction	Never or Almost Never			Sometimes			Often or Always		
Dreamer	1	2	3	4	5	6	7	8	9
Complainer	1	2	3	4	5	6	7	8	9
Brooder	1	2	3	4	5	6	7	8	9
Joker	1	2	3	4	5	6	7	8	9
Charmer	1	2	3	4	5	6	7	8	9
Explainer	1	2	3	4	5	6	7	8	9
Avoider	1	2	3	4	5	6	7	8	9
Actor	1	2	3	4	5	6	7	8	9
Tackler	1	2	3	4	5	6	7	8	9
Believer	1	2	3	4	5	6	7	8	9

on each scale on the questionnaire on page 167. Remember, your friend is to give an opinion of how he or she thinks *you* handle stress. Remember, too, that a 1 represents the least frequent reaction, while a 9 represents the most frequent.

Questions to think about and discuss:

1. What are the major stresses in your life right now? Write down a list of these and share part or all of the list with the group or with some other person who is significant to you. How many of your stresses come from relationships with others? Which come from frustrating events in your life? How many are caused by inner turmoil and hurts?

2. In dealing with your present stresses, which of the ten reactions have you used?

3. Look over the questionnaire you filled out. Which reactions do you use most often in dealing with stress? List the three most used.

_____ _____ _____

4. Is there a difference between your friend's evaluation and yours? If so, how do you explain the difference? Discuss these differences with the friend who rated you.

5. What makes it easy for you to react to stress in your three favorite ways?

6. Of the three sources of stress (relationships with others, frustrating circumstances, inner turmoil), which one gives you the most trouble? Why?

7. How does this chapter help you to understand others?

8. How would you hope to change as a result of reading *Give Me a Break* and completing this growthbook?

HOW MY FRIEND THINKS I HANDLE STRESS

Type of Reaction	Never or Almost Never			Sometimes			Often or Always		
Dreamer	1	2	3	4	5	6	.7	8	9
Complainer	1	2	3	4	5	6	7	8	9
Brooder	1	2	3	4	5	6	7	8	9
Joker	1	2	3	4	5	6	7	8	9
Charmer	1	2	3	4	5	6	7	8	9
Explainer	1	2	3	4	5	6	7	8	9
Avoider	1	2	3	4	5	6	7	8	9
Actor	1	2	3	4	5	6	7	8	9
Tackler	1	2	3	4	5	6	7	8	9
Believer	1	2	3	4	5	6	7	8	9

Conclusion:

The first step in understanding how to change is to be aware of who we are and what we do. Hopefully, this first chapter will help you see the origins of stress, understand how you deal with it, and prepare to discover how you can manage stress more effectively.

2

People Stress: Getting Along With Others

Much of life is spent around people—and that sometimes creates a lot of stress. It isn't easy to understand others (especially when they don't understand us). Misunderstandings and communication breakdowns occur, even among the best of friends. Prejudice, disagreements, and tensions appear in every corner of society, including high schools, youth groups, athletic contests, and other places where teens are in contact with one another.

In chapter 2 the author gives some basic principles for reducing "people stress" and shows how we can learn to get along with others.

To reduce people stress each of us should ask ourselves, *To what extent am I a part of the problem?* We should try to see the other person's point of view; work to improve communication, especially through listening; try to reduce other pressures and distracting influences; recognize God's power to help; and learn to accept the fact that some conflicts will not disappear.

Growth Projects

Reading about people stress can be helpful, but it helps even more if we can look at ourselves and see how the author's suggestions can be applied to our own lives.

Let's begin with some questions that are listed in the book. Take a few minutes to jot down answers to these questions.

- What are the people-problems in your life right now?
- What are you doing to make matters worse?
- Answer the following questions honestly. When you disagree with someone, do you
    —yell?
    —make sarcastic comments?
    —use belittling gestures?
    —make faces at others?
    —refuse to cooperate, listen, or talk?
    —stubbornly refuse to forgive?
    —demand your own way and refuse to cooperate?
    —expect that others will?
- How could you respond differently next time you have a disagreement with someone?

After you have answered these questions honestly, share your answers with one other person in the group.

After a few minutes, listen while the group leader reads the following paragraph:

> Close your eyes and pretend that you are a parent. Think about all the things you have to do in life. Think of the problems you have at work and at home. Think of the hassles of paying bills, fighting traffic, handling phone calls and interruptions all day.
>
> Now imagine that you have finally settled down in the evening for a few minutes of peace and quiet.
>
> Suddenly, without warning (and probably with no intention to

create problems), your teenager comes bounding into the room and turns on rock music—*loud.*

As a parent, what would you think? How would you feel? How might you respond?

What have you learned by looking at things from another person's viewpoint?

Questions to think about and discuss:

1. Think of a time recently when you had a disagreement with another person. Describe this to the group. Based on your reading in chapter 2, how could *you* have handled the disagreement differently? The group members should be invited to give their points of view on your people-problem and how it could have been (or could be) resolved.

2. In what ways does being a Christian help you to deal more effectively with other people?

3. Do you agree that some conflicts will never disappear? How do Romans 12:18 and Proverbs 15:1 apply to you?

Conclusion:

"People stress" isn't very pleasant, but God often uses these tensions to help us grow (*see* James 1:2–4) and to make us strong (2 Corinthians 12:9, 10). He also gives us the wisdom to deal with stresses (James 1:5), including the stresses of getting along with others.

It takes time, effort, and work to learn how to really get along with others. Once we learn this, however, we have gone a long way toward the goal of coping effectively with the stresses of life.

3

Peer Stress: Handling Pressure From Others

Other people can put us under a lot of pressure. Most of us discover this long before we become teenagers, but it seems that peer pressure is especially intense during the high school years. It is hard to say no when friends urge us to take drugs, break rules, or do other things that we know are wrong. Even when other people say nothing, the teen who wants to be accepted (and that includes just about everyone) often feels pressure to dress, talk, act, and even think like the other kids at school.

Consider Tim, for example. He got a job at a hamburger place and liked both the work and the money. But his boss and fellow employees teased him perpetually because he didn't take drugs, didn't jump into bed with the other kids after work, and went to church on Sunday.

In the chapter on peer stress, the author mentions four common ways of handling pressure from others. We can *cop out* and pull away from others; we can *compete* in sports, school, or other activities; we can *conform* to others and do what they expect; or we can learn from the pressure and use it to help build *Christian maturity*.

If we want to rise above the peer pressure and still get along well in this world, Chapter 3 suggests that we

- expect the pressure, so that it doesn't come as a surprise;
- resist the pressure, with God's help and the help of our real friends;
- counteract the pressure, replacing it with something better;
- avoid the pressure, whenever this is possible; and
- confess our failures to God whenever we give in to the pressure.

Growth Projects

Sometimes when we think in advance about examples of peer pressure, we are better able to handle the pressure when it comes. Consider, for example, the case of Sara.

Sara's biggest problem in life was algebra. It didn't make any sense to her, and the teacher showed a lot of impatience—even annoyance—on the two occasions when Sara went to ask for special help.

Two days before the final, Sara was told that somebody had "found" a copy of the exam. A lot of the kids had seen it, and a friend urged Sara to look it over. "It's dumb not to look!" the friend said. "You have problems with algebra anyway, and to look at the exam would be a sure way to pass and be done with algebra forever. This won't be unfair to the other kids since they've all seen the exam. If you don't look, you're sure to flunk since everybody else will do well."

What should Sara have done in response to the peer pressure? If you are meeting in small groups, each person may want to share an example of peer pressure from his or her own experience. Use one of these examples *or* use the case of Sara to consider the following questions:

- When peer pressure comes along, how do you usually respond? Give an example.

- When you give in to peer pressure how do you feel?
- Chapter 3 lists five ways of meeting peer pressure (expect it, resist it, counteract it, avoid it, confess it). How could Sara have used these to respond to the pressure from her friends?
- Should Sara—or you—ever tell a teacher or other adults about the pressures that come from peers? What are the advantages and disadvantages of discussing specific peer pressures with (a) your friends, (b) your parents, and (c) the people who are putting you under pressure?

Questions to think about and discuss:

1. Look up 1 Corinthians 10:13 and read it out loud. Does this have anything to say about your peer pressure?

2. Now look at 1 John 1:9 and discuss how this applies to you.

3. Based on your reading and discussion, how will you deal with peer pressure in the future? Be specific. Write down an answer to this question and then share your answer with the group.

Conclusion:

Without friends, life would be dull and self-centered. The same friends who give us encouragement and pleasure, however, can also put us under pressure and create havoc in our lives.

The Bible never encourages us to be hermits who withdraw from other people. Friendships are satisfying and important, but when friends put us under pressure, it is good to know that Christians are not alone. We have others who can help us with peer pressure, and—best of all—in Jesus we have a Friend who sticks with us, guides us, and never leaves or forsakes us, even when we feel pressured.

4

Chemical Stress:
What to Do About Drugs
and Alcohol

Why do teenagers take drugs?

A lot of adults wonder about this and shake their heads in amazement when they see kids drinking or "spaced out" on drugs. Teens, it seems, are less amazed about the widespread use of drugs or booze, but even some high schoolers wonder at times why so many kids become chemical "burnouts."

Chapter 4 suggests five reasons for teenagers' drug use. People drink or take drugs because of the example set by parents, the pressure from other teens, and/or the buildup of stress in life—this accompanied by the urge to find something that will bring even temporary relief. Some teens take drugs as a way of getting even with parents or school officials, and a lot of people use chemicals in an attempt to escape from boredom and the inner emptiness of life.

Probably few teens are impressed with horror stories about people who were killed while drunk or who died while high on drugs. It is easy to laugh at reports about the dangers of drugs, and most of us ignore stories of people whose brains have been damaged by chemicals.

When we are alone, however, or talking to some trusted friend, it makes sense to ponder what drugs really do. Very few people intend to become alcoholics or burnouts, but the slow influence of chemicals takes over and ruins thousands of lives every year. It makes sense then to ask, *Will it happen to me? How can I handle stress and live a meaningful life without destroying myself by chemical use? Can I help a friend who has a drug or drinking problem?*

These are good questions to think about, especially now when drug use is so widespread. Almost every teen must ask repeatedly, *What do* I *do about drugs and alcohol?*

Growth Projects

Start out by looking at the chart on pages 46 and 47 of your book. Columns 6, 7, and 8 might be of special interest. Can someone explain the meaning of words like *euphoria, delusions, convulsions, apathy,* or *disoriented*? Have you seen any of these symptoms in your friends? How could you make use of this chart in the future?

A lot of people take drugs in times of stress. For a while drugs and alcohol can dull the pain, but what are some of the long-term harmful effects of chemical use?

Let's be honest. If it hasn't happened already, at some time you probably will be tempted to "try out" some drugs or alcoholic beverages. How will you respond? How have you responded to such temptations in the past? Can you share your answers with the group?

Let's assume your little brother or sister asks you, "Is it okay for me to take drugs or to drink?" Write a one-paragraph letter to your brother or sister. Take the time to do this now—and be honest in what you write. We won't require anyone to read his or her letter, but would you be willing to share your letter with the group?

Questions to think about and discuss:

1. Have you or any of your friends tried to help somebody who has a drinking or drug problem? What did you do to help? Was your help effective? Based on what you have read in *Give Me a Break* (pages 54, 55), how can you help others in the future?

2. Think of the reasons people take drugs (parent pressure, peer pressure, stress, emptiness and boredom, a desire to protest). Which of these are most influential in your life? How could you meet these pressures and deal with them without taking drugs?

Conclusion:

Alcoholics Anonymous is a worldwide organization of people who are addicted to alcohol. These people have learned that drugs and drinking can be destructive influences. To keep from drinking, the members of AA have discovered that there is practical help to be found in praying about our problems and in reaching out to help others.

Each of us can get help from God and encouragement from others. We can understand ourselves better, know something about the dangers of drugs, and learn how to handle stress without using chemicals. It also can be helpful to everyone if we get into the habit of helping one another—even when there is no drug problem. Helping others is one of the best ways by which we can help ourselves to cope with *any* problem.

5

Parent Stress:
Crossing the Generation Gap

To be a teenager is to have problems with parents.

Moms and Dads often look at things differently than do their kids. Teenagers often want privileges parents are unwilling to give, and parents, in turn, can be disappointed and frustrated by the actions of their teens. Both parents and teens are learning to accept the fact that the teenager is no longer a "little kid," but neither are teenagers fullfledged adults with all of the responsibilities and bills which parents and other adults must bear.

Maybe the tensions between teens and parents are overexaggerated. In a lot of homes, families *do* get along fine, with only occasional "blowups." But this isn't true in every home—especially when the family members are under stress.

Give Me a Break shows that both teenagers and parents have pressures and other difficulties during the teenagers' high school years. Like their kids, parents too may feel frustration, financial pressure, discouragement, worries about the future, and a lack of understanding from the other generation. It helps, therefore, if family members can try to understand each other.

How can we understand one another and get along better? We can learn to be honest with one another, speaking the truth but always in a loving way (Ephesians 4:15). We can try—with God's help—to avoid explosions and angry outbursts of criticism. We can trust one another and show others that we are trustworthy. We can learn to listen and communicate. We can accept the fact that while some things may never change, this need not leave us in a state of despair. The Bible gives us hope for the future and shows that God is able to change even the most frustrating family situations.

Growth Projects

If you are reading through this book with a group of teenagers, you may want to invite all of your parents to the discussion this time. Somebody might summarize chapter 5 for those parents who didn't have the time or opportunity to read the chapter prior to the meeting.

Then look at the drawing on page 56. In what ways does this illustrate parent–teen problems in "crossing the generation gap"?

Each teen may want to interview his or her own parents or the parents of some other teen. How do these parents really feel about being parents of teenagers? What do they like and dislike about being parents of teenagers?

Before or during your meeting, each teen and each parent might be encouraged to write a short letter to each other. Teens could write what they appreciate about their parents; parents could write what they appreciate about their teenagers. Share the letters.

Think of the most recent time when you as a teenager had a major disagreement with your parents. How did you handle the issue? In what ways could it have been handled more smoothly? Discuss this with your group, your parents, or perhaps with another parent.

Many teenagers complain, "My parents don't trust me." Make a list of things you could do to show parents that you can be trusted. What would your parents add to this list?

Questions to think about and discuss:

1. What evidence do you have that your parents are confused, scared, inexperienced, and (most important) loving? How do they show their love? How do you show love and appreciation?

2. How do you respond to this quotation from the book: "You cannot make your parents change. . . . But what you can't do, God can."

3. Do you think Colossians 3:20 and 21 applies to teenagers?

4. How does Hebrews 12:15 apply to parents and teens? Read this in a modern translation.

Conclusion:

It is easy for parents and teens to concentrate on each other's faults, but this doesn't help anybody much. Instead, we can learn to understand each other, to communicate honestly and lovingly with each other, to respect one another, and to look for the good points in each other (*see* Philippians 4:8). In time, things probably will get better, but if they don't—in spite of your best efforts—then learn from these experiences so you can be a better person, and parent, in the future.

6

Family Stress:
Getting Along When Your Family
Falls Apart

Have you ever seen those little signs that look like this?

Maybe there are houses where all is quiet, serene, and secure, but even in the best homes, it seems, there is some tension—often mixed with frustration and disagreement. Nobody knows how many homes are characterized by almost constant arguing, nagging, and sometimes physical violence. Then there are homes dominated by sadness, grief, fear, poverty, sickness, or sometimes the constant threat of divorce, incest, beatings, or alcoholic stupor. It helps at times to think how good your home life is when compared with some other families in the neighborhood.

But to know that somebody else is suffering more doesn't do much to help us feel better. It can help to understand *why* families have problems, however, and that is how chapter 6 begins. It is suggested that family problems come because we all tend to be self-centered; we often don't know how to communicate; outside influences—like sickness, relatives, or the loss of a job—can put us under tension; and sometimes family members simply do not know how to resolve their differences of opinion.

All is not hopeless, however. It may take a long time, but with God's help, families often learn to get along better. At times, however, parents do separate and get divorces, or family members die. So sometimes teens have to adjust to grief, step-families, rejection, or the pain of a family member's alcoholism, child abuse, or problems with the law.

This chapter may not be pleasant to read and ponder, but it it realistic and helps you to face and handle some of the pain of family stress.

Growth Projects

What are the main problems in your family? Write these down and then share your list with one other person. What can *you* do to live with and solve these problems?

Do you know any teen whose family has been disrupted by divorce or death? How did the teen react? How could he or she have handled the stress better? How could you have helped? In what ways can you help now? Be specific.

It has been suggested that some issues create problems again and again in families. Look at the following list and decide which issues create tension in your family. Circle one number in each row.

Issue	Creates no stress		Creates some stress			Creates a lot of stress	
Lack of money	1	2	3	4	5	6	7
Use of the car	1	2	3	4	5	6	7
Time on telephone	1	2	3	4	5	6	7
Sickness of a family member	1	2	3	4	5	6	7
Parents arguing	1	2	3	4	5	6	7
Parents nagging	1	2	3	4	5	6	7
Child abuse	1	2	3	4	5	6	7
Brothers and sisters fighting	1	2	3	4	5	6	7
Grief over a family death	1	2	3	4	5	6	7
Problems with relatives	1	2	3	4	5	6	7
Self-centered family member	1	2	3	4	5	6	7
Alcoholism	1	2	3	4	5	6	7
Others (write in)							
_____	1	2	3	4	5	6	7
_____	1	2	3	4	5	6	7
_____	1	2	3	4	5	6	7

Now look over your list. On which items did you circle 4, 5, 6, or 7? What can be done to handle each of these issues? Be specific, then share your answers with the group.

Questions to think about and discuss:

1. In the Bible, the words *one another* appear almost sixty times. Look, for example, at 1 Thessalonians 4:18, 5:11, 15, and Galatians 6:2. How could these verses be applied to make things better in your family?

2. What are some specific ways in which you can help another teenager whose family is having problems? How could another teenager help you?

3. What do you think about the slogan that when a family prays together, they stay together?

Conclusion:

It isn't easy to handle family stress, and it's even harder to reduce that stress and to solve family problems. Getting along at home requires patience and understanding, mixed with a willingness to listen and to compromise. Remember the final words of chapter 6, "You can try to find ways to solve the problems. You can talk to God about them, knowing that He is aware of the situation and able to work in people's lives to bring change. That may be the most comforting idea of all."

7

Self Stress:
Learning to Like Yourself

Stress doesn't always begin with other people. Sometimes it starts inside ourselves—with our own feelings of inferiority, inadequacy, and self-criticism.

Chapter 7 begins by quoting Dr. James Dobson who has suggested that in order to feel good about themselves, many teenagers think they need at least three things: good looks, intelligence, and money. Most of us lack at least one (and sometimes all three) of these.

So how do we handle our feelings of inferiority? We avoid the "poor-little-me" way of thinking, we keep things in perspective so that we aren't overwhelmed by our assumed inferiorities, we get involved with other people, and we try to avoid self-defeating activities—like always putting other people down or boasting in an effort to convince others (and ourselves) that we really are worthwhile. In addition, there is value in challenging our own thinking—especially when we catch ourselves saying things like "I am stupid and ugly." Finally, each of us can work to develop the strengths and abilities we've got.

Growth Projects

Let's begin by taking stock of our strengths and abilities. On a separate piece of paper list

- five things you have done successfully in the past and enjoy doing,
- five things you can do well or could do well if you had some training or experience,
- five things that you have difficulty doing and enjoying,
- five positive traits about yourself (e.g., "I am kind," "I am patient"), and
- five traits that you need to work on (e.g., "I am lazy," "I am too critical").

Show the lists to a friend to get his or her reaction.

What do you dislike most about yourself? Based on your reading of the chapter, write down some things you could do to change your actions, thoughts, or attitudes. Share this with somebody else in the group.

Do you think it is wise to keep comparing yourself to others? As a group, discuss some practical ways by which you can learn to like yourself more. Does this have to lead to pride?

Questions to think about and discuss:

1. Chapter 7 states that God loves us and can help us to like ourselves better. Do you agree? How does being a Christian help you to like yourself better? Do Christians tend to have poorer self-images because they are Christians?

2. Do you know someone with the problem of anorexia nervosa? Such people need professional help—but what can you do as a friend to help them?

3. What do you think of the idea that most teenagers need three things to feel good about themselves: good looks, intelligence, and money? Is it possible to like yourself if you don't have these things?

4. Does sin interfere with your ability to like yourself? What does 1 John 1:9 say about this?

Conclusion:

When God created us, He made us in His own image and declared that His creation was good. Even after sin entered the world, God sent His Son Jesus to take our punishment—because God loves us and wants the best for us. Of course, nobody is perfect, but most of us are not as bad, incompetent, or ugly as we think. Even with our flaws, we are valuable people who can serve God and others with the abilities and energies we have.

It's true. The God who created us doesn't make junk!

8

Emotional Stress:
Handling Your Feelings

Everybody has feelings.

Sometimes we are able to keep feelings hidden, even from ourselves, but at times we all feel excited or disappointed, happy or sad, enthusiastic or bored. Some have suggested that emotions like these may be stronger and felt more intensely during the teenage years.

So what do we do with our feelings? According to the book, we begin by admitting that it is okay to have feelings and that it can be unhealthy to squelch our emotions. Then we work at handling our feelings by thinking before we express them and trying to deal with the people or problems that are causing the emotions.

To help make these ideas clearer, the book discusses several common teenage emotions. Discouragement and the kind of depression that can lead to suicide often come because we are physically run-down, concerned over some kind of loss, bothered by feelings of helplessness, or just plain angry. Fear comes when we are uncertain about the future or about some situation we might be facing. With these and other emotions, it helps to admit how we feel, talk things over with a friend, try to change our circumstances, and bring our emotions to God in prayer.

Growth Projects

The following is a list of some common teenage emotions. There is even space to add a few more if you wish. Please go through and put a check mark (√) next to each emotion, indicating whether you experience the feeling never, sometimes, often, or all the time.

I feel:	never	sometimes	often	all the time
accepted	___	___	___	___
afraid	___	___	___	___
angry	___	___	___	___
anxious	___	___	___	___
apathetic	___	___	___	___
bashful	___	___	___	___
bold	___	___	___	___
bored	___	___	___	___
clumsy	___	___	___	___
compassionate	___	___	___	___
competent (capable)	___	___	___	___
confused	___	___	___	___
cowardly	___	___	___	___
cranky	___	___	___	___
disappointed	___	___	___	___
discouraged	___	___	___	___
effective	___	___	___	___
embarrassed	___	___	___	___
enthusiastic	___	___	___	___
excited	___	___	___	___
friendly	___	___	___	___
guilty	___	___	___	___
happy	___	___	___	___
hateful	___	___	___	___
helpless	___	___	___	___
impatient	___	___	___	___
important	___	___	___	___
incompetent	___	___	___	___
inconsiderate	___	___	___	___
insecure	___	___	___	___
joyful	___	___	___	___
jumpy	___	___	___	___
laughed at	___	___	___	___
like laughing	___	___	___	___
lonely	___	___	___	___
loving	___	___	___	___
misunderstood	___	___	___	___

I feel:	never	sometimes	often	all the time
pessimistic	___	___	___	___
run-down	___	___	___	___
sad	___	___	___	___
selfish	___	___	___	___
unappreciated	___	___	___	___
unfriendly	___	___	___	___
unpopular	___	___	___	___
unwanted	___	___	___	___
weak	___	___	___	___
weary	___	___	___	___
worried	___	___	___	___
_____	___	___	___	___
_____	___	___	___	___
_____	___	___	___	___

Now go back through the list and look at the emotions you feel "often" or "all the time."

- How do you express these feelings?
- Do you ever discuss them with others?
- How could you handle these emotions better?
- Are some feelings hard for you to admit? Which ones? Why are they hard to admit?

Discuss these questions with someone else in the group. Show this other person your list.

Questions to think about and discuss:

1. Do you agree that "it's okay to have feelings" and that "it can be unhealthy to squelch feelings"?

2. Has it occurred to you that Jesus expressed emotions? Look up Matthew 21:12–17, Luke 22:39–46, and John 11:30–37. What can we learn from these examples? Do you think Jesus ever laughed?

3. How can you help other teenagers when they are discouraged, angry, or afraid?

Conclusion:

For the Christian, no emotion is more important than love. Jesus said that love should be the chief characteristic of His followers (John 13:34,

35), but most of us have times when we don't feel very loving. It is then, especially, that we need God's help, not only to make us more loving but also to help us deal with all of the emotions that come into our lives.

9

Sexual Stress: Handling Your Hormones

Probably every teenager thinks about sex—and some teens think about it most of the time.

To some extent we can blame this on our hormones. When we reach the teenage years and begin to mature sexually, feelings and desires we have not known previously are aroused. Television, movies, magazines, popular music, and the conversations of our friends all stimulate our interest in sex, and for many teens sex becomes life's greatest source of pleasure and pressure.

Sex, of course, was created by God and He called it "good." God knew, however, that people would abuse sex and use it to hurt others and themselves. To help prevent this, He gave guidelines to help us control and express our sexual urges. He warned of the psychological and spiritual dangers of sexual intercourse apart from marriage, and He gave guidance for expressing our needs for intimacy, acceptance, and love.

The book gives some suggestions for controlling sex, and it discusses ways of handling the guilt that comes when we give in to our sexual temptations. The chapter ends with discussion of a common concern of teenagers—masturbation—and with consideration of a growing issue in our society—homosexuality.

Growth Projects

Take a few minutes to think about one or two of the biggest struggles you have in the area of sex. It isn't necessary, and it may not even be wise, to share your struggles with someone else in the group (you may want to talk later with a youth leader or same-sex friend); but keep your personal struggles in mind as the group considers the following two issues. Be sure to get the reactions of your adult discussion leader.

1. How can we show concern and love for others, without being involved sexually?

2. Since everyone else is "doing it," does it make sense to wait until you are married for sexual intercourse?

Now turn to pages 111 and 112 and look over the guidelines for controlling sex. Write down how you could plan to change in the next few days. Tuck this paper in your wallet where others will not see your decision. Then as a group, ask God to help each of you to live with your hormones in a way that is pleasing to Him and good for you.

Questions to think about and discuss:

1. How can teenagers avoid sexually arousing situations without cutting out all of their fun?

2. Look over the section on guilt (pages 113 and 114 of the book). How can you handle guilt over sex?

3. The chapter ends with a quotation from 1 Corinthians 10:13. How does this apply to you?

Conclusion:

It is easy to reach the conclusion that sex was designed to dominate our thinking and to make life miserable for the people who really want to show some self-control. But sex was created by God as something to be appreciated and enjoyed, and God even gave us guidelines for enjoying sex to the maximum. Has it ever occurred to you that people who can't control their sexual urges are not free at all? They are slaves to their own lusts; and in the long run, such slavery is never good.

10

Religious Stress: Thinking Through the Things You Believe

- Does it really make sense to be a Christian?
- What do you think about hypocrites in the church?
- How do we deal with our questions about religion?

These are important questions for teenagers, and they are not easy to answer. We live in a time when a lot of people go to church, but their religion doesn't mean much personally. Self-centered thinking is very common; it isn't popular to spend a lot of time thinking about God. "I've decided to put religion on the shelf for a while," a teenager said recently. His thinking may be very common.

But questions about religion influence how we will live in this world and the next. Religious issues influence our standards of right and wrong, our friends, and even some of our ways of handling stress.

Chapter 10 raises important questions about religion and gives some answers. The chapter talks about hypocrites in the church and gives suggestions for handling the pressures that come to those people who are honest enough to think about their beliefs.

It can be painful and risky to face your questions honestly, but learning to handle religious stress can also bring great benefits in terms of peace of mind and meaningful living.

Growth Projects

Listed below are some religious issues that teenagers face. Read through the list and put a check mark next to the three issues that concern you most. When everyone in the group has done this, take a tally to see which topics are of greatest concern to the group members.

How can each of these issues be handled? As you ponder this alone or discuss it in the group under the direction of the group leader, you may want to take notes in the space on the right.

Notes

___1. I don't have any good reasons for believing in God.

___2. I have doubts about the biblical account of creation.

___3. I wonder if the Bible really is the true Word of God.

___4. I feel guilty for not telling others about my faith.

___5. I have difficulty resisting temptation.

___6. Church bores me.

___7. It bothers me that there are so many hypocrites in the church.

___8. Religion doesn't seem to apply to my personal concerns and problems.

___9. I'm afraid my friends will criticize or even reject me if they know I am religious.

___10. I can't see how I can be religious and still become independent of my parents.

___11. Religion doesn't make sense.

___12. Other: (Write it in)_____

_____

_____

___13. Other: (Write it in) _____

_____

_____

Questions to think about and discuss:

1. Look at the picture on page 119. Do you have any reactions?

2. It has been said that people today talk freely about sex but are reluctant or afraid to discuss religion. Is this true? Why?

3. Look over pages 127 and 128. Are these the best ways to deal with religious stress? What would you add?

4. Turn to 1 Timothy 4:12 and 2 Timothy 2:15. Do these verses have anything to say to you?
5. Look at Matthew 1:1–4. Is this example of Jesus helpful to us?

Conclusion:

In writing to his young friend Timothy, the Apostle Paul stated that all Christians who desire to live godly lives will be persecuted (2 Timothy 3:12). That isn't easy to accept and neither is it pleasant to think about. But the last sentence in the book is also thought-provoking. It may seem easier to "put religion on the shelf for a while," but this can lead us into "a phony religion with empty ritual or—even worse—into the futility and meaninglessness of the me-generation."

11

Future Stress: Finding Some Direction for Life

As a class project, a high school senior once did a survey of teenage stress and wrote her conclusions in a report for the school paper. Students feel pressure from their parents, according to the article. Students feel pressure from their peers and often students put pressure on themselves.

One of the big sources of pressure from parents, peers, and ourselves is the struggle of deciding how to plan for the future. It may be that in finding some direction for life we really are facing four very important questions:

- Who am I? (What is there about me that is unique?)
- Where am I going? (Do I have goals for the future?)
- How do I make choices? (Do I have some guidelines for knowing God's will for me?)
- What can I do now? (Must I sit around waiting for the future to unfold?)

Growth Projects

Chapter 11 gives several practical suggestions for planning your future. Look for examples on page 133. Take the time to fill in the blanks.

On page 137 the author lists eight important questions concerning your future direction. On a piece of paper, write your answers to the first six questions. This will take some time, but when you are done, share your answers with someone else and get his or her reaction. As suggested, keep the paper so you can add more ideas later.

As a group, discuss how one finds information about jobs and careers.

Your group probably includes some people who now have part-time jobs. Ask these people to share what they have learned about finding and keeping a job.

Questions to think about and discuss:

1. Chapter 11 suggests that we can find ourselves through religion (pages 134, 135). Does being a Christian help you face the future? Look at Jeremiah 1:5; Galatians 1:15, 16; Romans 8:16, 17; Romans 12:3–8.

2. Four suggestions are given for determining God's will. What are some of the decisions group members will have to make in the future? How can the four guidelines from pages 139 and 140 apply to your decision-making?

Conclusion:

It is sad to think about those Australian kids who have no hope for the future. But they are not alone, and even those of us who are more optimistic sometimes have problems even thinking of where we might be in five or ten years.

God doesn't often give clear messages concerning the future. Most often we must use our brains to find where God is leading. The believer can know, however, that God does and will lead in His own quiet ways. Proverbs 3:5, 6 is worth reading.

12

Teen Stress:
Guidelines for Managing Pressure

Sometimes it is helpful to end a book (and a discussion group) by summarizing what one has learned and putting everything together into a plan of action for the future.

That is the theme of the last chapter where ten practical guidelines are presented for any person who really wants to handle stress. When pressure builds up, we read, it is helpful if we can

- admit it,
- pray about it,
- analyze it,
- look at it,
- decide what to do about it,
- avoid self-defeatist reactions to it,
- back away from it,
- talk about it,
- learn from it, and
- reach out from it.

After discussing each of these, chapter 12 concludes with a sad but inspiring true story about a young man named Terry Fox. He faced incredible stress, but he rose above it and served his country even in the midst of great pressure.

You too can give yourself a break and manage the pressures of life effectively.

Growth Projects

Think of the time in life that was most stressful for you. You may want to share this briefly with the group.

If you can't think of such a time in your life (or even if you can), please read the following story and imagine that Pat is really *you*.

Pat is a high school senior, considered by most of the other kids to be a capable, friendly, and likeable person. Although neither brilliant in academic work nor outstanding as an athlete, Pat nevertheless has tried hard and has had a successful high school career.

But graduation is approaching, and Pat is faced with many pressures. There is school work to be done, the yearbook work to get completed, activities at church, a part-time job, a dating relationship which has been going well, and the pressure from parents to make a decision about next year. "Where are you going to college?" they have asked. "Have you completed the application forms? Do you have enough money? And why are you so seldom home anymore?"

Pat really wants time to slow down, to be alone to think, and to get some rest, but life has become fast-paced and, at times, almost frenzied.

Is this what college will be like? Pat wonders. *How can I reduce this pressure?*

Using the guidelines from chapter 12, decide as a group how Pat could reduce or otherwise handle the present stress.

Does chapter 11 present guidelines that might be practical?

How could you help someone like Pat?

Now that you have read the book, write down the three major stresses in your life. How can the ten points of chapter 12 help you to handle these pressures? Share your conclusions with someone else in the group—but don't reveal your three stresses unless you want to.

Questions to think about and discuss:

1. Now that you have read the book, in what ways will you handle stress differently in the future? Try to be specific.

2. We have all heard that prayer changes things. Can it change your stress?

3. As you conclude this book, why don't you pray about your pressures right now? Pray alone or with others in your group.

Conclusion:

When your parents were teenagers, few people heard words like *pressure* or *stress*. It has always been difficult being a teenager, of course, but in the past, people rarely talked about the stresses of teenage life.

Now, however, *stress* and *pressure* have become popular words. It is widely recognized that stress can be a powerful and destructive influence in our lives, and thousands of people have become interested in learning how to cope with stress.

Perhaps the best time to learn is when we are teenagers. Certainly the best help comes from God. That's the message of *Give Me a Break*. If you are learning that now, you are well on your way to handling the pressures of life with confidence and with skill.